LIVING *the* LORD'S PRAYER

THE HEART OF SPIRITUAL FORMATION

MORRIS A. WEIGELT
E. DEE FREEBORN

Beacon Hill Press of Kansas City
Kansas City, Missouri

Copyright 2001
by Beacon Hill Press of Kansas City

ISBN 083-411-903X

Continuing Lay Training Unit 112.13B

Printed in the
United States of America

Cover Design: Paul Franitza

Library of Congress Cataloging-in-Publication Data

Weigelt, Morris A.
    Living the Lord's prayer : the heart of spiritual formation / Morris a. Weigelt and E. Dee Freeborn.
        p. cm.
    Includes bibliographical references.
    ISBN 0-8341-1903-X (pbk.)
        1. Lord's prayer. I. Freeborn, E. Dee. II. Title.
BV230 .W36 2001
226.9'606—dc21

                                                                2001043869

10   9   8   7   6   5   4   3   2   1

Thanks be to God
for our wives,
for our children,
and for our students,
who have taught us
so much about
spiritual formation.

CONTENTS

FOREWORD

I t is often recited by worshipers at the table of the Lord's Supper, memorized by children in Sunday School, sung by soloists in countless weddings, and whispered by terrified soldiers huddled in harm's way.

Regardless of the circumstances, no portion of Scripture is quoted from memory more often than the Lord's Prayer. Indeed, this devotional treasure has linked denominations, generations, and cultures for nearly 20 centuries. The issues that frequently divide believers, such as biblical interpretation, worship styles, building budgets, and membership guidelines, pale when these words are sincerely prayed and practiced.

The primary reason for the prayer's monumental impact is that its contents are attributed to the Lord himself. Jesus was deeply concerned that His followers would maintain heartfelt communion with God. He instructed them to avoid hypocrisy and vain repetitions when they prayed. He then offered them a concise yet profound pattern to follow. From the first century on, these aptly chosen phrases have invoked reverence, repentance, and ultimate rest in the presence and providence of God. They have also become the source of innumerable sermons, songs, and books. And therein lies a dilemma.

An over familiarity with the Lord's Prayer can lull Christians to recite its words in a routine, mindless fashion. We are in danger of displaying the same superficiality that Jesus scorned earlier, in Matt. 6. That's why we need a fresh look at these poignant verses.

Our guides, Morris Weigelt and E. Dee Freeborn, are uniquely gifted for this divine enterprise. Academicians, students, and pastors throughout the Church of the Nazarene admire their genuine witness and careful scholarship. Together they lead readers on an inspiring pilgrimage that ascends way beyond "base camp" spirituality. Their grasp of the prayer's original Greek language, its rich meaning, and its relevance to today's Church offers life-changing insights. They are not nonchalant escorts who have conquered the summit, but fellow pilgrims eager to be transformed by this prayer's timeless truths.

As you explore the Lord's Prayer with this inspiring team, prepare to glean new perspectives about God, yourself, and others. It is likely you and the way you pray will never be the same.

With fervent mind and humble heart, let the journey begin.

—Janine Tartaglia Metcalf
Friend and *The Upward Call* coauthor

PREFACE

Welcome to our ongoing journey of inviting our Lord to teach us to pray until our praying and our living are totally integrated. Welcome to the ongoing journey of understanding personal and corporate spiritual formation.

In January 1983 we began teaching a course in spiritual formation for students at the Nazarene Theological Seminary "to supply the missing element in the curriculum." In 1989 we were invited to write articles on spiritual formation and prayer. In 1993 we were asked to teach a doctoral seminar on spiritual formation. The Holy Spirit led us to make the Lord's Prayer the core of the seminar. In 1994 we wrote, with Wesley D. Tracy and Janine Tartaglia Metcalf, *The Upward Call: Spiritual Formation and the Holy Life,* which was a survey of basic spiritual formation within the broader Wesleyan theological tradition. We trust this background helps you understand the burden at the heart of this volume.

As we accepted the challenge for this project, we faced a nagging question: Why another book on the Lord's Prayer?

Our dream is to fan a new fire of devotion and formational spirituality, inspired by the deep longings and sanctifying riches in the prayer our Lord taught us to pray.

So welcome to this book designed especially for you. Each chapter focuses on one petition of the Lord's Prayer. Each chapter also contains various items to illuminate the text. Scattered throughout the book you will find principles of spiritual formation especially highlighted. We trust these will be helpful to you in developing your unique walk with God.

In writing as partners, we faced the issue of using our names or personal pronouns. We realized that having team-taught for 18 years and having been friends for 47 years, we no longer know whose thoughts are whose. So for the most part throughout this book, we're using singular pronouns rather than indicating which one of us is writing or whose experience is being recounted.

If this book is of any value to you on your journey toward a deeper experience of Christlikeness, we will be most grateful and invite you to give praise to God, who made it possible.

Welcome to the journey! "Lord, teach us!"

—Morris A. Weigelt and E. Dee Freeborn

A word from our collaborating hymn writer, Ken Bible, who is an author, composer, music editor, and a friend of more than 25 years.[1]

Some years ago, the Lord challenged me to spend more time with Him in prayer and to use the Lord's Prayer as my guide. Not being a "liturgical" kind of person, I was surprised by the latter part of God's request. Nothing has changed and enriched my life more than this daily practice. I've come to use the Lord's Prayer as the framework for my daily prayer. I pray each petition, personalizing it and supplementing it for that day. Of all the changes this practice has brought in me, the most important is this: I focus less on my requests and more on worship and submission, refocusing on God and realigning with His will. And since singing is woven throughout my prayer life, this cycle of hymns on the Lord's Prayer arose naturally.

We are indebted to Ken for the original hymns that appear at the beginning of chapters 1 ("Teach Us to Pray"), 7 ("Our Daily Bread"), 12 ("Father, Your Name"), and 13 ("Our Father in Heaven").

ACKNOWLEDGEMENTS

We owe a great debt to a wide variety of people for their input in this material. We wish to thank the focus groups from the Canada Atlantic and the Washington Pacific Districts' pastors' and spouses' retreats who responded to individual chapters. We wish to especially thank the members of the "Spiritual Formation of Servant Leaders" module (January 2001) at Nazarene Theological Seminary who helped field test this book: Dwayne Adams, Richard Blodgett, Ron Brush, Jennifer Couchman, Tim Crump, Marcia Dean, Geoff DeJager, Merideth Densford, Brad Fink, Tom Gray, Mark Hatcher, Michael Hazlett, Stephen Hicks, Daryl Ireland, Cisca Ireland-Verwoerd, J. J. James, Roy Johnson, Lester Jones, Garry Light, Curt Luthye, Donnie Miller, Ajay Muktikar, Jerry Myhr, Nathan Patnode, Duane Pooley, Katrina Quick, Jennifer Showalter, Tony Sparrow, Dwight Sponagel, Shawn Stevenson, Soo Yeoul Suh, Joel Tooley, John Versaw, Mike Voudouris, Mark Watt, Kelli Westmark, Jason Worthington, and Jonathan Young. We're especially grateful for significant input of Dr. Roger Hahn.

We express special gratitude to Jeanette Gardner Littleton for her patience in editing our materials.

We also thank the following publisher for its kind permission to quote from its materials:

Oxford University Press and Lillenas Publishing Company for their kind permission to reproduce the words and music to Rosamond Herklots's "Forgive Our Sins As We Forgive."

Teach Us to Pray

Based on Luke 11:1

1. You called God Your Father and spoke to Him free - ly.
2. In liv - ing and dy - ing, You tho't of Him on - ly.

Je - sus, teach us to pray. Sub - mis - sive and
Je - sus, teach us to pray. Your prayer and Your

emp - ty, You trust - ed com - plete - ly. Je - sus,
pas - sion, His will and His glo - ry. Je - sus,

teach us to pray. And Lord, You were bus - y but
teach us to pray. When torn by the taunts and the

WORDS & MUSIC: Ken Bible

WEIGELT
Irregular

1

PRAYING AS BELIEVING
OUR LORD AND HIS PRAYER
AS A MODEL

*J*ennifer's[1] pastor invited her to participate in a leadership-training workshop centered on the Lord's Prayer.

The Holy Spirit pierced Jennifer's heart as the workshop leaders discussed forgiveness, an element of the prayer. Jennifer knew she had an unforgiving heart because of the way she felt her husband hadn't lived up to her expectations. In fact, she hated the sarcasm and bitterness she could see in her own life. Jennifer began to ponder what forgiveness could mean for the congregation, her own life, and her marriage.

Soon after the workshop, she went to her pastor's office to discuss the implications of the petition. As they prayed together, the Lord cleansed Jennifer of her festering bitterness.

A fascinating result occurred in her husband's life. As long as Jennifer had shown an unforgiving spirit, he felt justified in defying all she stood for spiritually. When he no longer had that excuse, he returned to church and to the Lord in search of forgiveness.

Serious interaction with the Lord's Prayer changed Jennifer's life and the quality of her marriage and prepared her to be a better leader. How and what we pray clearly reflects how we think and believe.

THE WAY WE PRAY REFLECTS OUR BASIC BELIEFS

Although we may talk a wonderful line in Sunday School class or over a cup of coffee, our praying more clearly reflects the thinking that guides our spiritual formation. When Henri Nouwen was teaching at Notre Dame, he invited students to submit written prayers for structural analysis and underlying theology. He recorded the results in *Intimacy*.

SPIRITUAL FORMATION PRINCIPLE 1
Spiritual Formation Is Nurturing
a Relationship with God.

> Write out your prayers for a week. What kind of an understanding of God do they reflect?

He discovered that a person's prayers reflected his or her understanding of God. Some students, for example, simply wanted God to clarify issues for them. Others saw God as a cosmic bellhop to fulfill their requests. Others even invited God to stop suffocating them.

The prayers also reflected their own self-concept in relationship to God. Their arrogance, confidence, joy, or fear was visible in how they expressed prayers.

> List your major ongoing prayer requests. With whom do you identify most—Peter, Rhoda, or the praying disciples?

Acts 12 provides a helpful example. The disciples were "earnestly praying" (v. 5) for Peter's release from prison. Their prayers were answered by miraculous intervention. When Peter arrived at the prayer meeting, the pray-ers could not believe their prayers had actually been effective. What an interesting theology that narrative reflects!

H. G. Wells wrote a parable about an archbishop who became so professional with prayer that he forgot how to really pray. One day, at the end of his rope, he decided to try praying again. After he said: "O God," a brisk voice responded, "Yes—what is it?"

They found his body the next morning sprawled on the crimson carpet. "But instead of the serenity . . . that was his habitual expression, his countenance, by some strange freak of nature, displayed an extremity of terror and dismay."[2]

This parable illustrates the essential connection between our belief system and our praying. What we believe about God and what we believe about ourselves will determine how we pray and the shape of our spiritual formation. In its base definition, spiritual formation is simply the way we develop a relationship with God.

- When we beg God to intervene but expect things to be exactly the same tomorrow, our prayers betray our real theology.

The way I prayed this morning showed I really did not expect an answer.
—Overheard at a workshop on the Lord's Prayer

- When we identify only items that we think God wants to hear, our prayers expose our understanding of God.

- When we ask God for a specific answer to prayer and then search for evidences that the answer is en route, our prayers reveal the quality of our faith.

- When we only hold seminars for God and never listen for His guidance, our basic beliefs not only restrict our praying but deeply affect our spiritual development.

> In your small group discuss the four bulleted statements. With which ones do you identify? Are there others you would add?

THE PRAYER LIFE OF OUR LORD AS A KEY TO HIS BASIC BELIEFS

Although we have records of fewer than 100 days of our Lord's three-year ministry, the Bible shows many references to His prayer life and His teachings about prayer.

Jesus' whole life and ministry grew directly out of what Edward Schillebeeckx called "his *Abba* experience."[3] At Jesus' baptism the voice from heaven announced, "You are my Son, the Beloved; with you I am well pleased" (Mark 1:11).

Jesus' prayer at Lazarus' tomb illustrates the quality of this relationship: "Father, I thank you for having heard me. I knew that you always hear me, but I have said this for the sake of the crowd standing here, so that they may believe that you sent me" (John 11:41-42).

A wide range of emotions is associated with His prayers. He prayed in joy (Luke 10:21); in turmoil (12:27); in distress (22:44); and in communion with His 'Abba' (John 17).

> Tell of an instance when you called upon God in a personal crisis.

Jesus advocated humility in prayer—witness the parable of the publican and the Pharisee. He advocated persistence in prayer—witness the parables of the friend at midnight and the persistent widow. He advocated expectant prayer in a variety of ways—for example, "Ask, and it will be given you; search, and you will find; knock, and the door will be opened for you" (Matt. 7:7).

His prayer at the Mount of Transfiguration was so profound that His disciples observed "the appearance of his face changed, and his clothes became dazzling white" (Luke 9:29).

The gospels record that Jesus prayed regularly, often in the early morning. Scriptures mention His search for places of solitude in which to pray. His teachings recommend a quiet place to pray to the Father, who sees in secret. Prayer is mentioned with reference to the great crises of His life: the temptation, the choosing of the Twelve, the Galilean uprising, upon His final departure for Jerusalem, in the Garden of Gethsemane, and at the Cross.

The "high priestly" prayer of John 17 also reflects the *"Abba"* experience. This prayer is after the Upper Room discourses, with Gethsemane just ahead. The first section of the prayer focuses on the mutual glorification ("The glory that I had in your presence before the world existed" [v. 5]) and unity of the Father and the Son. In the second section Jesus asked the Father to protect the disciples in turbulent days ahead as they were to pick up Jesus' mission. The basic beliefs of the Lord who prays stand out in bold relief.

> In a library or on the Internet, investigate books of written prayers to learn from the way others pray.

The Garden prayer, coming at the critical moment in Jesus' life and ministry, probably best demonstrates the integration of His praying and believing. The agony is nearly unbearable—Hebrews describes it as "loud cries and tears" [5:7]); Luke mentions sweat drops of blood, for the threat of impending death tests His deepest resolves. In prayer He once more realigns himself with Abba's will and rises resolutely to face the Cross.

His prayers on the Cross emphasize the coordination of praying and believing. Who can ever forget His request of the Father to forgive those who crucified Him? Or the prayer that the Father would receive His spirit?

Praying and thinking were so integrated that He could say, "The words that I say to you I do not speak on my own" (John 14:10). In the Garden our Lord demonstrated His fundamental belief system through prayer.

THE BASIC BELIEFS OF OUR PRAYING LORD—A SUMMARY

Perhaps the simplest way to summarize our Lord's teachings is to look at them through the lens of the Sermon on the Mount.

In his biblical theology of holiness, William Greathouse considers the Sermon on the Mount more important than the New Testament epistles, for the Sermon "spells out in detail what it is to 'have the mind of Christ' ('all the mind that was in Him') and 'to walk as He himself walked' ('not only in many or most respects, but in all things') (1 Cor. 2:16; see 1 John 2:6)."[4]

> For one week meditatively read Matt. 5—7 every day. Mark any passage brought to your attention by the Holy Spirit. Close by praying the Lord's Prayer.

Dallas Willard built his book *The Divine*

Conspiracy on the Sermon on the Mount. He says, "What we have come to call the Sermon on the Mount . . . concludes with a statement that all who hear and do what He there says will have a life that can stand up to everything—that is a life for eternity because it is already in the eternal (Matt. 7:24-25)."[5]

The Lord's Prayer is the core of the Sermon on the Mount. Tertullian wrote in the second century that the prayer is the gospel in brief. Simone Weil wrote, "The 'Our Father' contains all possible petitions; we cannot conceive of any prayer which is not already contained in it."[6]

> ### SPIRITUAL FORMATION PRINCIPLE 2
>
> Spiritual Formation Is Submission
> to the Lordship of Christ.

Let's look at an overview of these petitions.

"Our Father who is in heaven" (Matt. 6:9, NASB). The praying Jesus believed in a God of love and compassion who was accessible to His obedient children. He also believed in obedient sonship to the Father.

"Hallowed be your name" (v. 9, NASB): The praying Jesus believed that God needs to be revealed in our sinful world. He believed the holy love of a holy God can and must be illuminated and shared.

> What do you believe about worship in our culture today? Does praying and believing "our Father who is in heaven" make any difference? Should it? How?

"Your kingdom come" (v. 10, NASB): The praying Jesus had a vision of God's transforming kingdom. He went to the Cross to bring that Kingdom into full operation.

"Your will be done, On earth as it is in heaven" (v. 10, NASB): The praying Jesus believed that when God's name is hallowed and His kingdom erupts in the most unexpected places, His will is being accomplished.

"Give us this day our daily bread" (v. 11, NASB): The praying Jesus trusted the Father to supply every need—from bread for daily sustenance to the greatest spiritual gifts of grace.

"And forgive us our debts, as we also have forgiven our debtors" (v. 12, NASB): The praying Jesus believed that sin and evil do not have the last word. Our Lord voluntarily offered His life to bring reconciliation—vertical and horizontal.

"And do not lead us into temptation" (v. 13, NASB): The praying Jesus acknowledged that we find resources only in God to respond to life's temptations.

"But deliver us from evil" (v. 13, NASB): The praying Jesus understood the fractures sin has caused in our world. He asked for a divine intervention that would again hallow God's name.

> You may wish to copy this overview of the Lord's Prayer and carry it with you in your Bible or wallet.

"For Yours is the kingdom and the power and the glory forever. Amen" (v. 13, NASB): The praying Jesus believed "all our prayers are to God, and that we give ourselves along with our prayers to the divine keeping. Prayer begins and ends with God's own self; prayer is the offering of our own stories into the greater story that is God's drama with the universe, of which we are a part."[7]

What a prayer! What a gospel! What a life! What a theology! Jesus obviously prayed as He believed, and He believed as He prayed. He invites us to join Him in that same lifestyle and prayer style.

"Lord, Teach Us!"

Jesus' disciples began to understand the powerful integration of theology and His prayer life. According to Luke 11:1, they asked Him to teach them to pray as John the Baptist instructed his disciples. Jesus' disciples seemed to understand that prayer is a strategic clue to how a disciple lives out the Master's teachings. So they requested that He teach them to pray so specifically (within the larger pattern of the prayers of Judaism) that they would reflect His teachings and be identified as His disciples.

Our Lord taught His disciples to pray a profoundly simple prayer. This prayer—which should probably be more correctly called "the Disciples' Prayer"—contains only 38 words in the original Greek (as found in Luke).

It is a masterpiece of simplicity through which Jesus guides His disciples into praying in a manner consistent with His life and message.

At the heart of all praying is the Lord's Prayer. We need to hear that prayer at new depths to challenge the theological thinking at the core of our lives. With today's renewed interest in spiritual formation, the time to listen to the Lord's Prayer again has arrived.

2

PRAYING AS LIVING
OUR LORD AND HIS PRAYER
AS A MODEL

A grown son called his father to say, "Dad, I quit smoking. The doctor said if I quit now, my lungs would suffer no permanent damage."

"How, Jeff?" his dad asked, knowing Jeff smoked three packs each day.

"I knew it would be rough, so I made a vow to God that I would stop," Jeff said. "I figured I couldn't let God down. Every time I started to reach for a cigarette, I would say the Lord's Prayer. Sometimes I would say it 40 times a day."

Jeff stopped smoking, his faith was strengthened, and his health was enhanced. He still says the Lord's Prayer every night, "just to thank Him."

This story, told by the late Randall Earl Denny in sermons on the Lord's Prayer, illustrates the vital connection between praying and living.[1]

Though we can recite the Lord's Prayer in seconds, it deserves lifelong practice. It not only will change your prayers but also will change your life.

We can also illustrate the relationships between praying and believing and living in a diagram of a triangle.

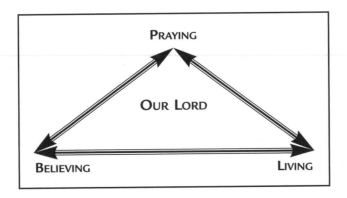

Our Lord is at the center of the triangle, symbolizing His centrality in the Christian's life. This also provides the model for our spiritual formation. The arrows between praying and believing, between believing and living, and between living and praying all point in both directions. These arrows express the reciprocal relationship between the way we pray and the way we think, between the way we think and the way we live, and between the way we live and the way we pray. When all three of these relationships are functioning in balance, we experience a vibrant Christian life.

THE SPIRITUAL FORMATION OF OUR LORD

During two decades of teaching spiritual formation, I have often contemplated the spiritual formation influences in our Lord's life. How did He develop such ideal balance between praying and living, praying and thinking, and living and thinking? What avenues of grace did He draw upon as our High Priest and Savior? Consider the following factors.

First, the quality of His relationship with the Father had a profound formative influence upon His life. I wonder how often He heard from His mother the story of His miraculous birth. At age 12 He was already thinking about being in His Father's house (Luke 2:49). The "Abba" experience of his baptism was deeply imprinted upon His life and ministry. The prayer at Lazarus' tomb (John 11:41-42) validates the quality of that relationship. His confidence that He and the Father were one (John 17:11) and His words and works were gifts to Him, for the Father certainly affected His spiritual development.

Second, His range of quotations from the Old Testament revealed that He knew His scripture. He developed a biblical mind-set that immeasurably affected His spiritual life.

Third, Jesus participated in the patterns and processes of His religious tradition. He repeated the Shema (Deut. 6:4) daily as prescribed. He attended the festivals of the Pentateuch. He attended synagogue and probably attended synagogue school (Luke 4:16). His longing to do God's full will was nurtured as He participated in His people's heritage. Who can comprehend the anchoring effect of these practices on His life?

> What is the role of the practices of your tradition in your personal spiritual formation?

A *fourth* factor in His development was His relationship with His spiritual friend, Isaiah. Even though they lived eight centuries apart, Jesus had spent so much time with Isaiah's writings that He quoted him at strategic moments of His life. He read from chapter 61 at His inaugural in Nazareth. He quoted from chapter 6 when opposition became so fierce that He turned to parables as a method of communication. He understood himself as the Suffering Servant through chapter 53.

A *fifth* factor was His involvement with the 12 disciples. He hammered out His thinking in those discussions. The relationships with the inner circle of that group are reflected in the Transfiguration experience and in the Gethsemane struggle.

> In your journal write a sentence/paragraph about what each of the elements means to you.

A *sixth* factor was His unqualified obedience to the Father. Hebrews says, "He learned obedience" (5:8). He did not wait to find out what was required of Him before deciding whether to obey. Jesus still experienced a struggle in the Garden, but lifelong practice prevailed, and He could say, "Yet, not my will but yours be done" (Luke 22:42).

Seventh, His redemptive involvement in others' lives had a profound formative effect. He offered love to all who came to Him—from the smallest child to the most hardened sinner.

> Discuss the eight influences on the spiritual formation of Jesus. Name any others.

Eighth, the consistency of His prayer life was a significant formative influence. Extending himself to those in need and renewing His heart and life in the Father's presence were regular rhythms in His life. The Lord's Prayer expresses the importance of His prayer life.

We could probably add many other factors to this list. Our Lord's model of carefully nurturing His spiritual life offers us direction in strategically developing our own relationship with God.

SPIRITUAL FORMATION PRINCIPLE 3

Spiritual Formation Is Enriched and Enabled Through the Cleansing Power of the Holy Spirit.

DEFINITIONS OF SPIRITUAL FORMATION

This book is designed to explore the deeper experience of Christlikeness through studying the Lord's Prayer and spiritual formation together.

The expanded working definition of "a deeper experience of Christlikeness" is this: *Spiritual formation is nurturing a relationship with God.*

Spiritual formation is (1) living the Lord's Prayer in everyday righteousness (2) through the enabling power of the Cross and the guidance of the Holy Spirit, (3) the whole person in relationship with God (4) within the community of believers, (5) growing in Christlikeness, (6) re-

In what ways do you nurture your relationship with God?

flected in a Spirit-directed, disciplined lifestyle, and (7) demonstrated in redemptive action in our world.

Let's explore this definition.

1. Spiritual formation is living the Lord's Prayer in everyday righteousness. The prayer patterns and quality of our Lord's living models the thought that praying and living are interrelated.

To pray as Jesus prayed in order to be identified as His servant is likewise a call to live out everyday righteousness as Jesus lived in order to be identified as one of His followers.

2. Through the enabling power of the Cross and the guidance of the Holy Spirit. Steve Shores wrote, "Many of us live as *if nothing decisive happened at the cross. We live as if we have to finish what Christ began.*"[2] Until our prayer styles and our lifestyles are integrated through the dynamic of the Atonement, our spiritual formation can hardly be designated as Christian. Until our lives are products of the Holy Spirit's guiding and enabling, they continue to be sub-Christian.

The radical optimism of spirituality is possible only because of the Holy Spirit's energizing and dynamic presence in the believer's life. "Apart from the grace imparted to us by God through His Holy Spirit, we are bankrupt and broken. Living by grace, we are freed to live a life pleasing to God, open to minister and serve those around us, ready to live in harmony with ourselves and our world."[3]

3. The whole person in relationship with God. Spiritual formation at its most fundamental level is a carefully cultivated relationship with God. From the opening words of the Bible, we clearly see God's call to relationship. The covenant language in the Bible underlines that call.

Draw a picture of your concept of God. Share it with a friend, or write a paragraph in your journal.

The Lord's Prayer points us back to the fundamental element of spiritual identity formation: a carefully fostered relationship with God from which all else in life flows. God is searching for people who bring every aspect of their lives to Him. Well-balanced spiritual formation flows from that fundamental perspective.

SPIRITUAL FORMATION PRINCIPLE 4

Spiritual Formation Is Growing Christlikeness.

4. Within the community of believers. The Lord's Prayer shocks us with the introductory pronoun "our." The petitions speak in the context of community: give *us*, forgive *us*, lead *us*, deliver *us*.

The Old Testament call to community is unmistakable. The New Testament builds upon that call. The Lord's Prayer teaches us that no lone rangers exist in God's kingdom. Jesus called His disciples together "to watch, pray, learn, live, imitate and practice the disciplines."[4]

5. Growing in Christlikeness. The holiness code of the Pentateuch already articulates this call to follow God: "I am the LORD your God; sanctify yourselves therefore, and be holy, for I am holy" (Lev. 11:44). The prophets continued this theme with urgency.

In the New Testament, the call to imitate God focuses on the life of our Lord, who can say: "If you knew me, you would know my Father also" (John 8:19).

Grace now makes Christlikeness a reality. Now the call to holiness of life is available to everyone. When we pray in concert with Jesus, a Christlike spiritual formation comes into view.

6. Reflected in a Spirit-directed, disciplined lifestyle. In two decades of teaching spiritual formation, I have seen that the Spirit-directed, disciplined lifestyle is as diverse in shape as the personalities God has given to us.

It would be interesting to have some of the people from Bible days hold a seminar on praying and living. I wonder how Paul and Peter would differ in their presentations. It would be intriguing to listen to Matthew and Mark debate on the topic.

God comes to us within the dazzling variety of our personalities and backgrounds. He expects us to come to Him through that same personality and background. So we join the early disciples in the request that our Lord teach us to pray and to live.

7. Demonstrated in redemptive action in our world. Maxie Dunnam wrote, "A spirituality that does not lead to active ministry becomes an indulgent preoccupation with self, and therefore grieves the Holy Spirit and violates the presence of the indwelling Christ."[5] As we surrender to

> In what ways are you involved in Christian redemptive action in your world?

God's redemptive designs, we are drawn back to the center to find strength and resources.

THE "SIMPLIFICATION" PROCESS

The complexity of elements in spiritual formation and the profundity of the Lord's Prayer can overwhelm us. I would like to propose a method of approach to the Lord's Prayer that I call the "simplification" process.

The idea for this process came from Leo Tolstoy's story of three monks who lived on an island in the ocean. They were so simple that they knew how to pray only *O God! You are three; we are three. Have mercy on us! Amen!*

One day the bishop arrived in his boat to give these simpletons a seminar in prayer. Upon completion, he headed back for the mainland. As he was congratulating himself on enlightening those poor monks, a ball of fire approached, skimming over the ocean. When it came to the boat, the monks disembarked. They had come to thank the bishop for the lessons on prayer but were afraid they had already forgotten them.

The stunned bishop, noting their mode of transportation, shook his head and told them to return to the island and continue praying in the same "simple" way they had prayed before his seminar.

If we could uncomplicate our lives enough to live and pray only the way our Lord taught us to pray and live, what kind of spiritual formation would result?

STRUCTURAL DIAGRAMS OF THE LORD'S PRAYER TO AID UNDERSTANDING

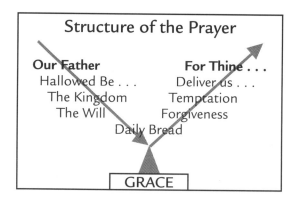

In working with the "simplification" question, it will be helpful to understand the pattern and structure of the whole prayer. Here are two different diagrams of the basic structure and direction of the prayer.

The first depicts the literary structure of the prayer in the shape of the letter *V*. The petitions on the left side of the "V" all focus upon God— His name, His kingdom, and His will. The petitions on the right side of the *V* are all related to our needs. The prayer opens with the invocation and closes with the doxology. At the pivot point of the *V* is the petition

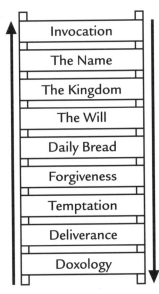

Invocation

The Name

The Kingdom

The Will

Daily Bread

Forgiveness

Temptation

Deliverance

Doxology

for daily bread—a petition that points to the centrality of grace in all spiritual formation.

I call the petitions on opposite sides of the *V* "complementary petitions."

A second diagram that can help us understand the overall structure of the prayer is that of a ladder. Our Lord instructed us to pray by ascending the ladder of prayer to gaze over the banister of heaven until our eyes and mind and heart are filled with God and His grand design. Then we descend trusting in His sustenance to find the daily bread we need and begin functioning as redemptive agents in our world.

Now we're ready to turn to the individual petitions of the prayer.

May God himself guide us as we follow our Lord in praying, thinking, and living. May we become instantly identifiable as His followers! In the name of the Father and of the Son and of the Holy Spirit. Amen!

SPIRITUAL FORMATION PRINCIPLE 5
Spiritual Formation Is Living the
Lord's Prayer in Everyday Righteousness.

3

"OUR FATHER WHICH ART IN HEAVEN"
AN INVITATION TO A RELATIONSHIP OF INTIMACY AND AWE

H annah was only 10 years old. Her mother and father seldom took her to church. One day she asked her grandmother to help her find the Lord's Prayer and copy it into her notebook.

A few days later she asked her grandmother to help her copy it again, since she had lost it. Then, for a third time, she asked for something else important in the Bible to copy.

When her grandmother asked her why she was interested in the Bible, she explained, "My friend Corinne doesn't know Jesus, so I taught her the Lord's Prayer and introduced her to Him. Now I need something else to teach her."

Just as Hannah introduced her friend to Jesus through the Lord's Prayer, Jesus introduces us to God through the opening words of the Lord's Prayer.

THE SETTING IN WHICH JESUS COMPOSED THIS PRAYER

The history of the Jewish/Christian faith could be visualized in terms of a pendulum swing between intimacy and awe—between transcendence and immanence. During some eras, the emphasis upon the sovereignty and transcendence of God seemed to remove Him from interaction with His human family. Like a cosmic Grand Canyon, the distance between God and His people seemed almost too great to bridge. Overstress on God's sovereignty leads us to a paralyzed paranoia.

In time, the pendulum swings in the other direction, and humans begin to assume a relationship of intimacy and even manipulation with reference to God. Their prayers no longer reflect the mystery and awe, and they address God in more human terms. Their flippant familiarity borders on disrespect.

In the four centuries before Christ's coming, mystery and awe ruled. Some said the Lord had given no prophetic word for over 400 years. In that period a great deal of emphasis upon angels had developed to bridge the gap between the transcendent God and the all-too-human earthly family.

In such a period of transition, our Lord taught His disciples to pray with a balance of intimacy and awe, of approachability and mystery. That balance—neither familiarity nor paranoia—is crucial to spiritual formation.

THE MEANING OF "FATHER"

Now Jesus balances the grand transcendent prayers of His own tradition with the intimacy of a father-child relationship with the Father.

It is no accident that the very first word in Greek is the word "Father." Failure to understand the connotation of this word will flaw the exposition of the whole prayer.

For Jesus, the Old Testament tradition is the immediate source of His understanding. The designation of God as Father was directly related to the understanding of the covenant. "God showed himself to be Father to Israel by acts of saving power in history."[1]

> In a Bible dictionary read about "covenant" to deepen your understanding of this term.

The prophets repeatedly returned to the motif of covenant faithfulness as the stabilizing force in a chaotic world. That faithfulness involves the highest degree of compassion. In Hos. 11, after recounting the repeated rebellions of Israel, the poet quotes God as saying, "How can I give you up, Ephraim? How can I hand you over, O Israel?" (Hos. 11:8).

> In the Old Testament God is called "Father" only 14 times.

In the New Testament the concept of "Father" takes added meaning in light of our Lord's relationship with the Father. The Son and Father have a unique quality of relationship.

The relationship of the Son to the Father is most clearly visible in the area of obedience. The Son was the ultimate servant, because His obedience was explicit and implicit. According to the Gospel of John, Jesus said, "The words that I say to you I do not speak on my own; but the Father who dwells in me does his works" (14:10).

> Meditate on the meaning of "Father" as the One being addressed—rather than as the subject of a sentence.

The high priestly prayer recorded in John 17 demonstrates that our Lord enjoyed the quality of relationship with the Father to which He is inviting us in the Lord's Prayer. The reality of this promise is visible in verses 21-23 of this prayer: "As you, Father, are in me and I am in you, may they also be in us, so that the world may believe that you have sent me. The glory that you have given me I have given them, so that they may be one, as we are one, I in them and you in me, that they may become completely one, so that the world may know that you have sent me and have loved them even as you have loved me."

> What areas of your life reflect obedience functioning well? What areas need attention?

So Jesus' use of the word "Father" is not "sloppy fraternizing" with God. He comes to obedience the old-fashioned way, because He trusts the Father's covenant faithfulness, tender mercy, and great compassion.

> What would it mean in your life to "learn obedience through suffering"? Are you willing?

A Revolution in the Meaning of "Father"

The simple word "Father" in Jesus' mouth and at the opening of the Lord's Prayer brings a radical revolution in our understanding of God and the quality of our relationship with Him.

The human concept of "father" does not become the model by which God's fatherhood is understood. Rather, all of biblical history pours content into the term. And in no place is the essence of the Heavenly Father more visible than in His giving His only Son for our atonement.

We must always remember that Jesus invited us to join Him in this special quality of relationship with the Father. He is our older brother indeed—and only His authority makes such an approach viable.

> Name a time when God significantly answered prayer for you. Did you record it? If not, why not start a prayer journal?

Frederick Buechner observed that we could dare to pray the remainder of the prayer only if God were that kind of Father. It takes courage to be bold enough to pray the radical petitions that follow. "To speak these words is to invite the tiger out of the cage, to unleash a power that makes atomic power look like a warm breeze,"[2] he states.

God as Father knows the end from the beginning and offers us guidance in our confusing world. He is the "Father in heaven" whose resources are endless—and eternal. What a joy to belong to a God like that! He responds to our spoken and unspoken needs!

THE MEANING OF "OUR"

The second word in the Greek text (and the Latin and Spanish) is the word "our." To pray "Father ours" reveals another critical dimension to the prayer. Why did Jesus teach His disciples to pray in the plural?

German theologian and preacher Helmut Thielicke said we find the first significance of the plural in the person who invited us to pray in this way. Although Jesus' name is never mentioned in the Lord's Prayer, we never pray this prayer alone—"It is Jesus Christ himself who teaches us to pray the Lord's Prayer."[3]

> Using the alphabet as a guide, make a list of descriptors of God. For example:
> A—almighty;
> B—beautiful

He has opened up "the new and living way" (Heb. 10:20) into the Holy of Holies, into God's very presence. He now invites us to share that access and use the word "our" with Him.

The plural then also broadens our perspective to help us recall that we never pray alone. We pray in concert with the whole Body of Christ. This theme appears repeatedly in the Lord's Prayer.

"Our" and a Sense of Belonging

Another implication of this crucial second word of the Lord's Prayer is the sense of belonging. When we acknowledge God as our Father, we also confess a sense of belonging. We discover Him as our Creator, our Source of grace, our Source of salvation, our Source of guidance and direction—our Source of everything. In a world shattered by sin and broken relationships, we need a place to belong. We are no longer isolated by the sabotage of sin. We have a God who cares and understands.

The sense of belonging embraces all those who own Christ as Lord around the world. That's why we feel an instant bond when we meet a Christian of another culture.

The writer to the Hebrews helps us see that the sense of belonging transcends time. In chapter 11 he tells of the great heroes of the faith. He begins chapter 12 with "since we are surrounded by so great a cloud of witnesses" to show that we belong with all the saints who have ever lived. What marvelous company! What a powerful influence! As if being at a jubilant family reunion, no one can exclude us—we belong!

The possessive "Our," while it expresses our sense of belonging, never becomes negatively possessive. In no sense do we own God or expect to manipulate or direct Him. We have access to this privilege of approaching God only because of what God has first done for us through our Lord Jesus Christ. We are the beneficiaries of God's work on our behalf.

The person who prays in the plural is clearly an individual before God but an individual with Kingdom membership. Individuality is never lost in uniformity.

> Describe a time in your life when you experienced a healthy sense of belonging or a strong sense of worth.

THE MEANING OF "IN HEAVEN"

When we add the final phrase of the invocation, "in Heaven," the intimacy is balanced by the mystery and the awe. We have already noted that we are recipients of His unmerited grace. Now we acknowledge God as the Creator. The Apostles' Creed confesses God as "Maker of Heaven and Earth." Any over-familiarity we may have assumed suddenly vanishes.

To understand that God has a location, "in heaven," frees us to pray on a universal level. Willimon and Hauerwas declare, "We are bold to pray for such absurdly extravagant gifts as bread for the world, peace among nations, healed marriages, cured cancer, rain . . . because we pray to the Father in heaven, the one who rules."[4]

We recognize that our life is now a part of God's grand design. We can endure setbacks and sufferings, because we participate in a larger world.

When Jesus taught His disciples to live as they pray and pray as they live through the Lord's Prayer, He was inviting them to a relationship in which intimacy and mystery are appropriately balanced.

> In your prayer practice, how do you nurture the awe and the mystery?

The invocation of the Lord's Prayer has profound implications for our spiritual formation. As we daily acknowledge Him as our Father in heaven, we place ourselves in a context to be molded by grace. This stance of submission allows God to work in and through our lives as part of the larger redemptive pattern.

Thanks be to our Father in heaven!

SPIRITUAL FORMATION PRINCIPLE 6

Spiritual Formation Is Learning to Listen to the Wisdom.

Hallowed Be Thy Name

(Matt. 6:9-13)

Adapted from Scripture

Traditional West Indian Melody
Arr. by Lyndell Leatherman

4
"HALLOWED BE THY NAME"
THE PETITION OF TOTAL ABANDONMENT

*I*n the 1960s, when the Republican National Convention nominated Richard Nixon for the United States presidency, the headlines of one newspaper proclaimed, "The Greatest Comeback Since Lazarus." Today that reference would be meaningless to the average audience.

We live in a biblically illiterate culture. The phrases of the Bible no longer make sense to a majority of people.

The blurring of boundaries and structures in this rapidly changing culture make it difficult to find images that communicate. New words, such as "chaordic" and "glocal," are being invented on a daily basis—and lose meaning as rapidly.

> What evidence of lack of acquaintance with the Bible do you see in the culture? Do you see any in yourself?

The search for a stable center in such a fractured world is increasingly difficult. It helps to recall that our Lord also lived in an age of dramatic shifts and in a politically oppressed environment.

The First Petition

In a similar setting, our Lord taught His disciples to pray "Hallowed be your name!" This is a stabilizing and radical prayer for any age. In the invocation, Jesus established that a relationship of intimacy and mystery form the core of spiritual formation. There is the mystery of being invited to communicate with the creator God of the universe.

The primary response to the instability and frightening speed of change in our culture is found in total abandonment to God, to whom we pray. The contract must hold no fine print—no loopholes for exit in case we find ourselves in difficult circumstances. This directive of our Lord coincides with the biblical call for us to completely consecrate ourselves to God in order to find fulfillment.

INSIGHT FROM STRUCTURE

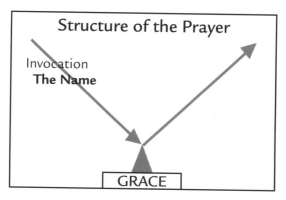

This first petition becomes even more radical in light of its relationship with the invocation. What kind of a God would invite His people to address Him in the imperative voice, or with a forceful command?

We might have expected the verbs to be interrogative—questions that politely request God's intervention. Instead, we find imperatives that reflect a rich quality of relationship with the Father.

> Why does God need us to pray for His holiness to be revealed?

The fact that the Lord's Prayer occurs at the center of the Sermon on the Mount in Matthew suggests that only people who try to live every aspect of this sermon are in the position to speak in such commanding tones to the Father. Only people in whom the Beatitudes are functioning on a daily basis may bring their requests so boldly to the Creator.

> In what ways has God revealed His holiness and love in unmistakable ways to you? Through you?

The other surprise is to understand that God even *expects* us to urgently request that He hallow His name. Our Lord teaches us to approach our heavenly Father with a stringent request that He proceed to make His name holy—in our lives, in our families, in our churches, in our city, and in our world. Just what are we daring to demand?

THE MEANING OF "NAME"

In he original, the word "name" connotes title, authority, and power. In the Old Testament a name is always associated with the essence of the person. To know a person's name is to understand his or her personality.

This is illustrated by Jacob's change of names in Genesis. "Jacob" means to supplant, deceive, or attack from the rear. After his wrestling match at the Jabbok River, the Lord changed his name to "Israel"—"he who strives with God" or "Prince of Elohim." What a difference!

> If you were to become fully God-centered, how would your life change?

The primary essence of God's personality is presented in His name. In the Lord's Prayer our Lord invites us to ask God to hallow His name—to make His primary essence fully visible. If God's primary essence is love, then we are requesting that He make that love visible. If His primary essence is holiness, then we are demanding that He display that holiness. If His primary essence is holy love, we anticipate a full revelation of that holy love.

> In light of this petition, what is the appropriate physical and spiritual posture of someone who prays? For example, some pray face down, others on their knees, others standing with their hands raised.

Suddenly we see the seriousness of taking the Lord's name in vain. The wrongful use of His name contradicts a respect for His essential being.

THE MEANING OF "TO HALLOW"

Lev. 22:32 helps us understand the connotations of "hallow": "You shall not profane my holy name, that I may be sanctified among the people of Israel: I am the LORD."

Definitions of "hallow" include "set apart as sacred to God; make holy, consecrate; regard as sacred; purify, cleanse."

What does it mean to ask God to set His name apart in our world? What does it mean to ask God to consecrate His name or to purify and cleanse His name? What does it mean to request that God sanctify His name?

"Taking the Lord's name in vain . . . is the sin of living in contradiction to that holy name. To profane his name is to live in such a way that others are unable to know God as he really is."[1]

The other side of that truth then suggests that hallowing His name is living in such a way that the essence of God's nature is on display in how we act and talk and respond.

> List some ways believers display God's holiness in their daily lives.

The person who daily prays this prayer is expecting God to honor the petition and is also offering to protect the honor of that name. The person who has abandoned himself or herself to God through this prayer thus becomes a vehicle to display that presence.

Implications for Spiritual Formation

God Clearly Revealed

First, the person who prays this prayer daily is praying to a God who has a name and a location. God is no mere abstraction or a figment of one's mind. God has revealed himself through His actions and His words in scripture. The believer now expects further manifestations of His essential being.

> If you invited God to hallow His name, how would your life need to change?

God's Grace at Work

Second, the person who prays this prayer daily chooses to live so God's holy love will be visible in his or her life. When God's hidden holiness is displayed through the believer's life, he or she becomes an evidence of God's grace at work in a sinful, broken world.

> ## Spiritual Formation Principle 7
> Spiritual Formation Is Enabled by the Power of the Cross of Christ.

A Repentant Attitude

Third, the person who prays this prayer daily recognizes the ways in which his or her life has obscured rather than revealed God's true nature. The result is a repentant attitude for all of those moments of obstructing others' view of God.

Abandonment to God

Fourth, the person who prays this prayer daily, through the act of praying, offers his or her life in submission to God. That submission is an abandonment to God's design—a willingness to be used in His patterns and programs.

The person who gazes into God's face and offers himself or herself in total availability to Him realizes that His design far

> For each of the next seven days before you read your Bible, pray a prayer of intentional obedience. In your journal, record your responses to what God reveals to you in His Word.

outdistances the individual's own designs. Jesus taught His disciples to place themselves under God's guidance and control in their daily prayers.

Brendan, St. Patrick's disciple, adopted the motto: "Lord, help me raise my sail, and throw away the rudder!" That is the essence of abandonment to God.

Obedience to God's Call

Fifth, the person who prays this prayer daily offers himself or herself in total obedience to God's call. John Wesley invites people to pray a prayer of intentional obedience before reading the scripture—asking only that God provide directions, and they will already be en route to obey. The coupling of appreciative obedience and predetermined obedience has powerful formational effects.

> List ways you can be obedient to God tomorrow.

Subordination to God

Sixth, the person who prays this prayer daily starts with God's design. He or she does not pray to invite God to bless personal preferences. All personal preferences are subordinated to God.

In John 17 Jesus prayed for himself, His current disciples, and His future disciples. His orientation, however, is in the words of verse 11: "Holy Father, protect them in your name that you have given me, so that they may be one, as we are one."

Openness to God's Reordering

Seventh, the person who prays this prayer daily is prepared for the divine revelation that may disrupt personal plans. Jesus taught us to begin prayer and life by gazing first of all at God. This orientation makes a profound difference. In abandonment we find the greatest freedom—a freedom obtained only under the umbrella of a top-quality relationship with God.

> To what level of disease and dis-comfort are you willing to go in order for God's name to become fully visible?

When we invite God to hallow His name, we must be prepared to let Him change any things in our life to make His name become visible. Martin Luther wrote, "I know of no teaching in all of the Scriptures that so mightily diminishes and destroys our life as does this petition."

A REVOLUTION IN OUR UNDERSTANDING OF GOD AND HIS CALL TO HOLY LIVING

Only when we approach a God who is Father are we free to live out such a radical petition. Only recognizing the revolutionary understanding of God uncovered in the invocation enables us to dare to request that God reveal His hidden holiness so dramatically.

> ### SPIRITUAL FORMATION PRINCIPLE 8
> #### Spiritual Formation Requires Silence.

Some people are surprised the Lord's Prayer includes no petition inviting God to make us holy. Again, it is a matter of orientation. Martin Luther observed that a stone lying in the August sun does not need to be commanded to be warm. Warmth is the normal by-product of the relationship.

> Consider the proposal that one who lives in close relationship with God will naturally live a holy life. What are the implications?

The person who lives in close relationship with the Father and on a daily basis invites God to hallow His name will normally live a holy life in response. Then holiness of heart and life becomes a by-product of a top-quality relationship with God.

Paul discussed of God's display of glory in 2 Cor. 3 and 4. In the third chapter he argued that God's glory is vividly displayed in Christ's face. In the final verse of chapter 3 he stated that this glory is in the transformed lives of God's people. In chapter 4, verse 7, he wrote of the jars of clay in which that glory is displayed. The earthen pots are divinely designed never to detract from their contents—God's glory.

> List the elements of your life that will need organizing for you to live this prayer. Are you willing to face the conflicts that praying this petition will bring into your life? Write this commitment in your journal.

That descriptive chapter illustrates the result of daily praying that God's glory and person may be displayed in a broken world.

THE RADICAL NATURE OF THIS PETITION

This first petition of the Lord's Prayer is truly radical—seeming almost too radical for us to dare to pray. This revolutionary petition brings us into conflict with the primary standards of our culture.

It will call for us to organize all of our living and giving and praying and investing in terms of God's kingdom. That would be truly revolutionary.

To live the way we pray and pray the way we live will clearly identify us as servants of the Servant! Do you have the towel firmly in position and the basin of water ready?

5

"THY KINGDOM COME"
THE PETITION OF
RADICAL EXPECTANCY

Helmut Thielicke was preaching a series of sermons on the Lord's Prayer in Stuttgart, Germany, during World War II. His third sermon was built on "Hallowed be thy name." Before he could preach on "Thy kingdom come," American bombers destroyed the center of the city and most of the cathedral in which he ministered. He preached his sermon on this second petition in the choir loft—all that was left standing. His sermon began this way: "Isn't there a comfort, a peculiar message in the fact that, after all the conflagrations that have swept through our wounded city, a sermon can begin with these words: 'We shall continue our study of the Lord's Prayer?' We don't need to interrupt and search the Bible for texts appropriate for catastrophe."[1]

The structural sequence of the Lord's Prayer continues to amaze me. The invocation establishes a Bible-wide understanding of the God we serve. The first petition—"Hallowed be thy name"—asks that God shows the authentic understanding of His

> What did Jesus have to embrace in order to claim the Kingdom? What did He have to give up?

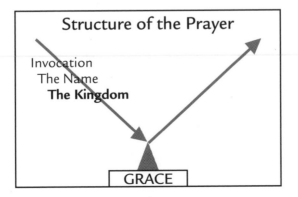

Structure of the Prayer

Invocation
The Name
The Kingdom

GRACE

essential being to a broken world. Now the second petition replaces the human understanding of "kingdom" with the divine perspective.

If we could pray and live the full meaning of this petition, it would revolutionize the way we deal with tragedy.

JESUS' UNDERSTANDING OF THE KINGDOM

Jesus used the word "kingdom" in the opening announcement of His ministry (Mark 1:14-15). This announcement implies that the period of waiting for the Kingdom is over. The Kingdom is no longer a distant hope but a present reality.

> How do you prefer to define "Kingdom"?

The records of Jesus' temptation found in Matthew and Luke imply that the wilderness testing of Jesus centered in issues of the Kingdom.

Satan offered our Lord shortcuts to Kingdom fulfillment, but Jesus was not interested. In fact, Satan offered Him "all the kingdoms of this world"—even though they were not his to offer.

Jesus had a vision of the nature of the Kingdom and the nature of a suffering servant. This vision enabled Him to resist Satan's approaches.

Jesus' inaugural sermon at Nazareth, according to Luke's record, interprets the Kingdom in terms of compassionate ministry. His vision that day was stated in the words of Isa. 61: "The Spirit of the Lord is upon me, because he has anointed me to bring good news to the poor. He has sent me to proclaim release to the captives and recovery of sight to the blind, to let the oppressed go free, to proclaim the year of the Lord's favor" (Luke 4:18-19)

> Who are the marginalized where you live? What does it mean for the Kingdom to be extended to them?

The power of that vision in our Lord's life is still visible when John the Baptist's disciples inquired whether or not Jesus was the expected Messiah (Matt. 11). Jesus responded again with the evidence of the Kingdom: "Go and tell John what you hear and see: the blind receive their sight, the lame walk, the lepers are cleansed, the deaf hear, the dead are raised, and the poor have good news brought to them. And blessed is anyone who takes no offense at me" (Matt. 11:4-6). John the Baptist and Jesus clearly held dramatically different understandings and expectations of the Kingdom.

While en route to His Triumphal Entry, Jesus stopped to heal the blind man, Barti-

> What kind of evidence do you need in order to believe the Kingdom is alive and well?

maeus, at the side of the road (Mark 10:46). He extended the Kingdom's compassion even as He moved toward the Cross.

THE NATURE OF THE KINGDOM

John the Baptist's question continues to be relevant. Just what is the Kingdom? What are evidences that it is functioning? When we pray the Lord's Prayer what do we expect to happen?

> How do you reconcile the fact of God's kingdom with the evil you see in the world?

When we face the question of the nature of the Kingdom for which we pray, we must always define it in terms of Jesus' teaching and ministry. Jesus understood that the Kingdom was actually breaking into the world with dramatic effects. Wherever Jesus went, people were transformed.

The language Jesus used in referring to the Kingdom demonstrates that it was not His but belonged to God exclusively. The phrase "kingdom of God" appears 52 times in the Gospels. Matthew, writing to a Jewish audience, prefers the phrase "kingdom of heaven." Jesus understood that He was the vehicle of accessibility to the Kingdom, but the Kingdom is where God reigns and rules.

> Why does Jesus sometimes use parables instead of declaration to teach about the Kingdom?

Dallas Willard in *The Divine Conspiracy* points out that the kingdom of God is much more than simply God's rule in individual's hearts. God is working out His will and design in the whole universe.[2] Jesus opens accessibility to that Kingdom to all who would become apprentices to His way of living and praying under God. Without arrogance He could say, "The kingdom of God is not coming with things that can be

> The word "kingdom" appears 148 times in the New Testament, with 114 occurrences in the four gospels alone.

observed; nor will they say, 'Look, here it is!' or 'There it is!' For, in fact, the kingdom of God is among you" (Luke 17:21).

Thielicke recognized that the forces of this world are contrary to the values of the Kingdom: "The manifestations of God's will are emerging ever more clearly and conclusively in the very midst of decline and decay, and God's sovereignty rules in power above all the rebels and usurpers, bringing his great and ultimate plans for the world to fulfillment."[3]

Jesus used a variety of picturesque language to convey the Kingdom's

> If you took this petition seriously, how would your life need to change?

boundaries. He used hints, analogies, parables, and imagery to describe the structures of God's kingdom. Let's look at a few of His most instructive parables to help us know what to expect when we pray, "Thy kingdom come."

In the parable of the mustard seed (Mark 4:30-32), Jesus informs His hearers that small beginnings don't mean the Kingdom is insignificant. When it breaks through in all its glory, it will provide shelter for all. The smallest seed becomes a great tree that shelters the birds of the air.

In the parables of the treasure in the field and the pearl of great price (Matt. 13:44-46), our Lord implies that the Kingdom is the highest priority on earth. It is worth the greatest expense and the highest sacrifice to obtain.

> List examples of what it means to "extend the Kingdom" to "the poor in spirit" in your world.

In the parable of the great banquet (Luke 14:16-24), Jesus states that the Kingdom is not for the privileged few, but extends to the disenfranchised and the nobodies in the world's eyes. The Kingdom is not a closed fellowship for the privileged, but an open society for any who will apprentice themselves to Jesus and join the Kingdom for which they pray.

In the imagery of the old and new wineskins (Matt. 9:17), Jesus declares that the dynamic of the Kingdom is so powerful it will no longer fit into old patterns. God is overthrowing the established religious world.

In the parable of the sower (Mark 4:2-9), Jesus prepares His followers for temporary setbacks. The parable also points to the magnificent victories in the Kingdom world—en route to the grand finale God has in mind.

KINGDOM EXPECTATIONS

This is indeed a "heady" petition to pray. It is a prayer of giant expectancy resting in faith upon the Creator—God of the universe.

G. C. Berkouwer writes, "The prayer 'thy kingdom come' is no stammering monologue, but a prayer that expects an answer. And every time we pray the Lord's Prayer there is reason to go and stand at the window of expectation."[4]

At one stage, some in the Early Church

> What small sign do you see as hope-filled evidence that the Kingdom is breaking in? How would looking for and rejoicing in the smallest signs of the Kingdom change your outlook on the challenges in your life?

recommended that so powerful a prayer as the Lord's Prayer should not be placed in the hands of unbelievers—it was far too dangerous to be handled by the inexperienced.

When you arise in the morning and pray the Lord's Prayer, what do you expect to happen? When you go to the window of expectation at the end of the day, what clues and signs are you looking for?

IMPLICATIONS FOR SPIRITUAL FORMATION

What are the implications of this second petition of the Lord's Prayer for spiritual formation?

In this petition we expectantly request that God's kingdom plans be brought to fruition. We see a shift away from the personal and selfish to God's grand design. To pray this prayer may call for me to smash my own kingdoms, that His kingdom might have preeminence.

SPIRITUAL FORMATION PRINCIPLE 9

Spiritual Formation Is Building the
Word of God into the Fibers of Our Being.

The Transforming Power of the Kingdom

A person's spiritual formation is changed because the boundaries have been changed. The familiar and divisive boundaries of this world are replaced by the redemptive boundaries of the Kingdom. Paul wrote in Gal. 3:28, "There is no longer Jew or Greek, there is no longer slave or free, there is no longer male and female; for all of you are one in Christ Jesus." All the boundaries are replaced by a new set of relationships and objectives.

> What personal kingdoms in your life will have to be smashed that *God's* kingdom may appear?

A powerful shaping influence grows out of these new relationships.

The Enabling Power of Praying for the Kingdom

When we anticipate the Kingdom, we find a new zest to life. We develop "Kingdom eyes" and see the smallest signs that the divine invasion is already beginning. One of my children once asked a sibling, "Why does Dad take the smallest sign as a signal that major breakthroughs are about to occur?"

That's normal for the person who has prayed for Kingdom victories to happen and is standing at the window of expectation. Elijah read the sign of the cloud the size of a man's hand as the indicator that rain was about to end a long period of drought (1 Kings 18:44).

> In your journal identify any experiences that have stolen your hope. Unmask that fear in the presence of the Risen Christ.

The Kingdom-oriented person celebrates the blessings of salvation, divine guidance, a stabilizing relationship with God, and the radical optimism of grace. These gifts—often thought to be available only in the final messianic age—are actually available and functional now. The perspectives of Kingdom people are totally changed.

Jesus taught us that Kingdom people are not destroyed by the terrors of the end time. These will not control the person who prays for the Kingdom. The new long-range perspective enables us to deal with chaos without being overwhelmed.

Near the end of his sermon on this petition, Thielicke wrote that he was peering into a bomb crater where 50 young men had been incinerated. A young woman joined him and observed that her husband had died in that pit. Only his cap was recovered by the cleanup squad. Then she turned to her pastor and said, "We were there the last time you preached in the cathedral church. And here before this pit I want to thank you for preparing him for eternity."[5]

People who pray with the Kingdom in view know that evil does not have the last word—and that knowledge profoundly shapes their lives.

Praying for the breakthrough of God's kingdom frees us from the fatalism that sucks the hope and life out of us. We recognize that God can use life's crushing experiences to shape us into redemptive vessels He can use. We know beyond the shadow of a doubt that God is in charge. Even in the darkest moments, we hear our Lord saying, "Now when these things begin to take place, stand up and raise your heads, because your redemption is drawing near" (Luke 21:28).

Daring to pray this petition with radical expectancy enables us to join the "search and rescue operation" for the King. We recognize the power of evil and sin. We know that many people are so trapped in the snares of the evil one that they need strategic help to break out. Like rescue teams in a catastrophic flood, we offer to "get down and dirty" to help them.

We dare to offer our Kingdom-enabled energies to others. We make such investments because we can see the Kingdom potential in the most disreputable people.

We recognize that living contrary to the values and preferences and patterns of this world will bring us into conflict with the powers that control it. We are not surprised by the conflict. We follow one who turned a cross into a plus sign.

The power of the Lord's Prayer is beginning to dawn upon us. We can no longer live parochial and provincial lives. We follow the King and walk to a different drumbeat. Each day we rise and pray that the Kingdom may break through. Each day we run to the window of expectation anticipating new evidence that the Kingdom is indeed coming. What a way to live!

The prayer "thy kingdom come" is echoed in the final prayer of the Book of Revelation: "Amen. Come, Lord Jesus!" (Rev. 22:20). The answer cannot come too soon!

6

"THY WILL BE DONE IN EARTH, AS IT IS IN HEAVEN"
THE PETITION OF PROACTIVE MISSION AND SUBMISSION

Forty years ago my (Morris's) college roommate and I were both young pastors in our first assignments. As we struggled to turn our education into application for our parishioners, we faced major threats to our own faith. His first child was born with life-threatening defects. My wife was dying of cancer, leaving me with the prospect of raising my two young daughters alone. We exchanged prayers and phone calls and long letters as we struggled with the issues. We corresponded about the nature of praying and the nature of God's will for our lives within the larger perspective of God's will. My friend articulated that wanting to find and do God's will was the highest priority of our lives—and not just because we were ministers.

> Describe a major setback in your life that made it difficult to submit to God's will. How was God's grace present in that situation?

So what does it mean to pray for God's will as our Lord invited us to pray in the Lord's Prayer? What do we expect to happen when we pray this third petition, "Thy will be done"?

> In your small group discuss the question: "What do we expect to happen when we pray this third petition?"

INSIGHTS FROM STRUCTURE

The structure of the Lord's Prayer again offers help. The prayer opens with a frank and exciting acknowledgment of the Father, to whom we pray. The first three petitions all focus on asking the Father to function as God in our world—to make His hidden holiness visible through hal-

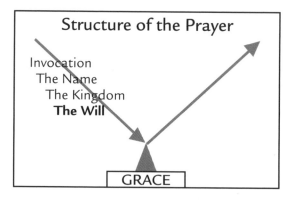

Structure of the Prayer

Invocation
The Name
The Kingdom
The Will

GRACE

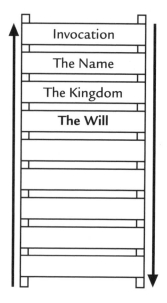

Invocation
The Name
The Kingdom
The Will

lowing His name, to multiply the Kingdom breakthroughs that demonstrate Jesus as Lord, and to accomplish His overall design en route to the final wrap-up.

We can visualize the structure of the Lord's Prayer to this point as a ladder. Each morning the person who seeks to be formed in the Master's likeness begins prayer by climbing the ladder and peering over the banister of heaven. Prayer begins by speaking in concert (remember the whole prayer is spoken in the plural) with Christians all over the globe, requesting that today be a day in which God will hallow His name, plant evidences of the Kingdom, and extend His saving will to more people and places and earthly kingdoms.

> In what areas are you being challenged to move out of your comfort zone? Name a specific step you can take to respond to that call.

INDIVIDUALISM IN CONTEMPORARY CULTURE

Princeton University sociologist Robert Wuthnow says America's yearning for the sacred has drawn the people into the community of small groups. But the individualistic focus has led them to choose among small groups. Wuthnow dubs it "the Goldilocks syndrome." Like Goldilocks of "The Three Bears" fame, they test the groups and decide which is too hard, which is too soft, and which is just right—and personal preference wins.

As a result of this emphasis upon the individual's role, this third petition of the Lord's Prayer is often interpreted in personal terms. A person can become obsessed with finding God's perfect will for his or her life. The larger perspective of God's overall will is lost in the drive to reach for our own best in life.

This search for God's perfect will is often tied to a rather fatalistic theology in which surrender means that God will force us to do what is most abhorrent to us—He will completely subvert our plans and force us to function totally outside of our comfort zone.

When we individualize this petition, we rob it of its essential content. To interpret it in personal terms contradicts the intent and flow of the whole prayer.

GOD'S SAVING WILL

G. R. Beasley-Murray analyzes this petition and writes: "In the context of a world actually wandering from God, it is His saving will that lies at the center of this petition."[1] The whole Gospel of Matthew, in which this prayer is found, reflects God's burden for a lost world. Our Lord commissions the Eleven in the final words of the Gospel, "Go therefore and make disciples of all nations, baptizing them in the name of the Father and of the Son and of the Holy Spirit, and teaching them to obey everything that I have commanded you. And remember, I am with you always, to the end of the age" (Matt. 28:19-20).

> In your small group read Ps. 46. Discuss the relationship of the psalm to this idea of God's saving will.

When we examine this third petition in the larger perspective of God's saving will, the tone and content change drastically. The petition, in the words of Rudolf Bohren, becomes a "missionary petition." God's saving will extends to all humanity. By praying this petition, God's people not only invite God to accomplish His will but offer to enlist in the mission. They are requesting that God work out His saving will in their lives, in the lives of their neighbors, and in the whole world.

> In what ways is God calling you to be involved in His saving will in your immediate world?

Our Lord's prayers in Gethsemane illustrate the overlap of the personal search for God's will and the universal flow of God's will. Jesus not only taught us to pray for God's will to be accomplished but also modeled praying it that terrible night in the Garden.

Jesus' own vision of the Suffering Servant from Isaiah taught Him

> Read Matt. 26:36-39. Picture yourself in the Garden. In your journal finish this sentence: If I were to take the Garden of Gethsemane seriously, my prayer life would be changed by . . .

that suffering and judgment would join at that crucial moment. In the agony of the hour (Matt. 26:38; Mark 14:36; Luke 22:44) He stated His preference that "If it is possible, let this cup pass from me" (Matt. 26:39).

He arrived at the moment of submission and submerged His will to the Father's design. So He prayed, "Yet not what I want but what you want" (Matt. 26:39). In verse 42 He uses the very words of the Lord's Prayer: "your will be done."

> Is there a "cup" in your life? How will you go to meet it? What part are you willing to allow God to play?

"An active, not a passive Jesus comes before us in preparation for His Passion. He does not resignedly capitulate to the darkness that comes upon him . . . At the end of the scene he is not on his knees passively awaiting coming events. He stands up, rouses his disciples, and strides toward decision, going to meet his betrayer."[2]

The prayer is so radical that it cost our Lord His very life. But as Thielicke notes, "That nocturnal struggler in the garden of Gethsemane uttered those words with a blessed sense of liberation."[3]

RESIGNATION OR RELINQUISHMENT?

A profound difference lies between resignation and relinquishment. In resignation we surrender to what we see as being inevitable and pray "your will be done" through clenched teeth. We struggle to the very end.

> In your small group discuss the difference between resignation and relinquishment.

When people pray the prayer this way, they reflect a less-than-Christian theology. They perceive God as an ogre who seeks to overwhelm and destroy. They assume that surrender will force them into disagreeable situations.

Relinquishment, however, assumes and presumes that God is the One revealed to us by our Lord—our elder brother. Relinquishing our wills to the will of such a God carries no unbearable burden.

When we tie together the promises of the Kingdom and the promises of God's will with the vision created by such promises, the sacrifices are no longer sacrifices. The joy of serving the larger vision enriches and enables all of life.

Paul illustrates this in 2 Cor. 4. He acknowledges the pain involved in following Christ but discounts the suffering in light of the glory of the New Covenant he described in chapter 3. He owns the "wasting away" of the outer nature in the process of fulfilling God's will but designates this as "momentary affliction" in comparison with "an eternal weight of glory beyond all measure" (2 Cor. 4:17).

> Is there any area in your life that's calling for relinquishment instead of resignation?

Adrian van Kaam distinguishes between reluctant abandonment and appreciative abandonment to God's will. Reluctant abandonment refers to the clenched teeth, last-ditch resistance that finds little joy in serving God. Appreciative abandonment is recognizing the wonder and joy of the divine design that brings hope and purpose and vision to life.

THE MEANING OF "BE DONE"

"Be done" carries a fairly broad range of meaning: to become, to be, to happen, to take place. Luther's translation of this phrase into German reflects a request for God's will to *appear* or *happen* on earth as it does in heaven.

> In your small group discuss what "a decisive display of God's will in our broken world" would look like.

The verb in the original calls for a decisive intervention. Our Lord taught us to pray for a decisive display of God's will in our broken world.

THE POSSESSIVE "YOURS"

The final word of the petition in Greek is "Yours"—a possessive pronoun. The position in the sentence emphasizes that only God owns the Kingdom. To pray this prayer is to submit to the Father, as revealed through our Lord Jesus Christ.

This third petition adds the phrase "in earth, as it is in heaven." In a sense, this final phrase of the third petition also applies to the previous petitions: *May the climactic and dramatic demonstration of the nature of your holy name appear here on earth as it does in heaven. May the breakthroughs of your Kingdom and will be visible on earth as in heaven.* And now we pray for God's decisive will to be revealed on earth—assuming this is already fully being done in heaven.

When God's will begins to come into view, as it has in these three petitions, the longing for a sin solution in this broken world becomes nostalgic. After all of the prayers I have prayed, I can't quite comprehend

> One of my responsibilities as a law enforcement chaplain involves delivering death notifications to homes, many with diverse religious backgrounds. In each home I use the Lord's Prayer to help the family through the early stages of the grief process. In one case, a young man had been killed in a car accident. When I tried to gently tell his family about it, they became hysterical. I began praying the Lord's Prayer with them. A sense of calmness settled over this family, and they began to heal in the midst of this tragedy. Once again I found the Lord's Prayer to be a source of great comfort to a family in the midst of tragedy.

how God will work out His design, but I have an assurance that He will. There is a homesickness that can hardly wait. We also feel a freedom that comes from not having to be able to comprehend it. What a joy it will be to come home for the first time—to the home where God's will will be final and finally done.

This longing for the heavenly tomorrow to become a reality does not exclude the struggles that will happen between here and there. The path to the final accomplishment of God's will still includes suffering—even as our Lord demonstrated. The prayer "Your will be done" is not pious dreaming of a sweet by and by. It is a call for the decisive advent of divine power.

IMPLICATIONS FOR SPIRITUAL FORMATION

So what are this petition's implications for spiritual formation? If you could simplify your life enough to only pray and live this petition, what kind of formation would be normal?

A clear God-orientation

The person who prays this prayer daily will have a short-term and long-term focus that is God-oriented. Immediate problems will be submerged into God's grand design.

A deeper understanding of God

To pray this petition is to be liberated from a paralyzing understanding of God. Such a freedom would be the opposite of the attitude of the young man who admitted that his favorite Bible verse was Heb. 6:4: "For it is impossible to restore again to repentance."

SPIRITUAL FORMATION PRINCIPLE 10

Spiritual Formation Is a Function of
Our Total Life's History.

A freedom from trying to control everything

Submitting to the divine vision frees us from the need to control everything. Surrender to God's control means we place trust in God to work through the dysfunctions and disgraces of life.

Freedom to throw yourself into Kingdom issues

People who live and pray as our Lord taught us will be freed to participate in pro-Kingdom "resistance movements" despite pressure they receive from earthly powers. Their spiritual 20/20 vision based on the radical optimism of grace will free them to love the unlovables of the world and help them find Kingdom lifestyles.

A freedom to pray with hope, patience, and joy

Such God-oriented and Kingdom-oriented people pray with hope, being convinced that God is fully in charge. They pray with patience, trusting God's timetable. They pray with joy, knowing the outcome does not rest upon their abilities. They are willing to pray in public to let the whole world know they march to a different drumbeat.

The finale to all truly Christian prayer builds from this petition. Whether we're praying for the terminally ill parent, for the drug-addicted person, for an unsaved child, for the salvation of a whole nation, or for the salvation of the whole world, we pray with a appreciative abandonment to His will. We outline the results we would like to see and trust the God who sees beyond our narrow ability to envision the results.

I challenge you to live the promise of praying and living God's will as your highest priority.

SPIRITUAL FORMATION PRINCIPLE 11

Spiritual Formation Is Personality Specific.

Our Daily Bread

Based on Matthew 6:11

♩ = 68

3rd time to Coda ⊕

Lord, to-day, just to-day,_____ Our dai-ly bread. Lord, from

You, just from You,_____ Our dai-ly bread. 1. All we want and all we
2. Like the man-na in the

need Can on-ly come from You a-bove, So we're rest-ing in Your
wil-der-ness, You give it ev-'ry day, So we walk with You by

D.C. ⊕ CODA

wis-dom, And we're lean-ing on Your love._____ bread._____
faith And as Your chil-dren sim-ply pray:_____

WORDS & MUSIC: Ken Bible

OUR DAILY BREAD
Irregular

"GIVE US THIS DAY OUR DAILY BREAD"
CONFESSING AT THE TABLE OUR TOTAL DEPENDENCY UPON GOD

Have you experienced the sense of surprise when a symphony transitions from one movement to the next? You've become involved in listening to the smashing forte rhythms of the overture, and suddenly you hear the adagio lightness of the second movement. It's the same symphony, but a different perception.

In much the same way, the transition from "Thy will be done" to "Give us this day our daily bread" surprises us. We are suddenly at the heart and center of the prayer. The whole prayer balances on this petition.

> Describe how it feels to pray for daily bread after completing the first three petitions.

INSIGHTS FROM STRUCTURE—THE NATURE OF THE SHIFT

The evidence for this shift is clear. A change from "your" to "us" moves the focus from God's grand design and His will to the needs of the disciples on earth, from "your name," "your kingdom," and "your will" to "our bread," "our debts," "our temptation," and "our need for deliverance." This includes a drastic movement from the petition that God's global will may become functional to our basic need for physical bread.

However, is this a shift in theme or just in perspective? On the surface, this petition appears to be straightforward. But the more we meditate upon its simple profundity, the

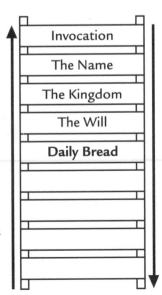

Invocation

The Name

The Kingdom

The Will

Daily Bread

more we realize it is a shift in perspective. It is a move from offering God our obedience to demonstrating our complete trust in His grace.

If we return to visualizing the structure of the prayer as a ladder, the shift does not appear as drastic. It may be because, as many commentators have pointed out, this is the complete prayer.

"The whole light of life is captured in this rainbow of seven petitions. Nobody can ever say that it sends him away empty-handed or that it does not take into account his need."[1]

> How do you understand bread as the central petition in the Lord's Prayer?

The focus remains upon God and His honor.

If we return to envisioning the structure in terms of the V-shape, then daily bread becomes the point at which the

> How does your prayer life identify you as a servant of Jesus?

divine and the human connect. If the essence of relationship between the divine and the human is the fundamental issue of grace, then daily bread becomes the pivot on which the whole prayer style and lifestyle of the follower of Jesus rests.

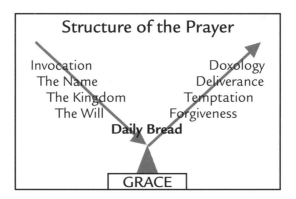

Structure of the Prayer

Invocation　　　　Doxology
The Name　　　　Deliverance
The Kingdom　　　Temptation
The Will　　　　Forgiveness
Daily Bread

GRACE

When the balance is lost in either direction, the quality of spiritual formation suffers. If the prayer style and lifestyle of the disciple overbalances on the human side (praying only for personal earthly needs), God is largely left out of the equation. If the prayer style and lifestyle of the disciple overbalances on the divine side (praying only for God's grand designs without getting involved in the messy side of living on earth),

> *There is so much beauty*
> *In bread—*
> *Beauty of sun and soil,*
> *Beauty of patient toil.*
> *Winds and rains have*
> *caressed it,*
> *Christ often blessed it.*
> *Be gentle*
> *When you touch bread.*
> —Author unknown

> When you pray this petition, do you normally think of bread as physical or as spiritual?

the disciple loses top-quality redemptive impact with the world in which he or she lives. Even the grammatical structure of the petition for daily bread (with the imperative verb in the middle of the Lord's Prayer) points to the pivotal nature of this petition.

INSIGHTS FROM THE TEXT

It's tempting to move this prayer immediately to the spiritual side and to ignore the material side. After all, isn't physical bread far too insignificant a petition in light of the preceding petitions? Does God care about the minor, daily things of life?

> Why do you think that the only miracle recorded in all four Gospels is the feeding of the 5,000?

Jan Lochman points to the high regard for eating in the Bible, to Jesus' use of earthy analogies to communicate great truths, and to the fact that Jesus is criticized for eating with the wrong crowd. He then observes

> In what ways could you make giving thanks at mealtimes more significant and worshipful?

that Jesus revealed himself to the disciples in Luke 24 through breaking the bread.[2]

"Obviously, the question of material bread is not marginal but central in the church's activities and prayers. The petition for bread rightly lies at the heart of the Lord's Prayer."[3] Jesus carefully taught us that the spiritual and material are integrally related to each other.

This seemingly simple petition "pierces the hidden darkness of our unexamined motives and values. It cuts with surgical precision to heal our foolish, culture-driven, anxiety-laden goals and aspirations."[4] It is the acid test of our commitment and theology. It is the point at which we demonstrate whether we depend on grace or not. It truly makes a difference how we offer thanks over our meals.

> The MRI machine was cold, stark, and forbidding. Pam was told to lie totally still during the entire operation. Her inner terror was even colder than the temperature of the room and the table. Suddenly Pam felt prompted by the Spirit to pray, "Give us this day our daily bread." As she repeated that simple petition, peace flooded her mind and heart and body. The gift of the divine presence in the loneliness of the test was more than enough. Thanks be to God!

"Bread": The Levels of Meaning

The word "bread" does have several levels of meaning in the Bible.

1. It is used most frequently for the physical bread that is the staple of every table and was especially so in biblical times.
2. Sometimes "bread" refers to the whole range of physical nourishment. Paul says in 2 Thess. 3:8, "We did not eat anyone's bread without paying for it."
3. When Jesus calls himself "the living bread that came down from heaven" (John 6:51), He is clearly promising sustenance beyond food.

All three levels of meaning are visible when Jesus lifts up the bread at that wonderful Last Supper and says, "This is my body, which is given for you. Do this in remembrance of me" (Luke 22:19). The Lord's disciples have understood all three levels of these meanings down through the centuries.

> How much bread is sufficient—whether you're thinking physically or spiritually?

"Daily" and "This Day"

The Greek word "daily" in "our daily bread" is found only in this one location in the Bible. It was five centuries before it was discovered in a list that seems to point to the meaning of "daily rations"—food that was necessary to pick up at the market each day in days before refrigeration.

Since the word "today" or "this day" also appears in the petition, the nuance of thought for "daily" leans in the direction of a quantity of bread. Then the petition is asking God to provide sustenance adequate for this day. We are instructed to trust God's adequate supply in the same way as the birds of the field and the grass and flowers of the earth do. Bread, as shorthand for grace, cannot be saved for the future. It is new and must be received daily.

> How would you defend the point that bread is really shorthand for grace? Or is it?

The story from Exodus of the manna in the wilderness provides a great analogy. We are invited to request bread and grace adequate to the needs of the specific day.

"Us" and "Our"

Even here—and especially here—in the petition for daily bread we always pray in community. The implications of this plural petition for the spiritual formation of the apprentices of our Lord are staggering.

If a person could trust God implicitly for everything in life, starting with sufficient bread for the day, how would life change?

A Growing Understanding of Who God Is

The petition for daily bread implies a simple faith in the God who provides. The mere request is an acknowledgement that the bread on our tables is given to us by God.

To arrive at a simple trust that God will provide is to acknowledge Him as the source of all things. He truly is the Father to whom we pray.

> In your journal: List the ways you and your family regularly acknowledge the truth that God is the source of all things.

Consider the story of the seminary students at a Trappist monastery. One student was so captivated with the taste of the bread that he dared to break silence and ask, "Did we bake this bread, or was it given to us?" One monk, taking pity on the student, simply replied: "Yes!"[5]

An Increasing Dependence upon God

Depending upon God's grace is a fine art, which has been damaged by sin in our lives. To return to dependency requires strategic practice.

> On the heavenly "trust meter" marked from 0 to 100 percent, where would you score?

It is so easy to claim dependence upon God theologically and conceptually, but much more difficult to live it out. So in a sense, our confession of dependency at mealtime is a dress rehearsal for confession of dependence in much larger issues. Recognizing God's blessings leads to an ever-increasing dependency upon Him.

A Greater Sense of Community in the Body of Christ

The person who regularly prays this petition acknowledges an essential connection with all those created by God. Every time we practice dependency at the table—whether in our home, at the fast food restaurant, or together in community, we acknowledge our dependence upon God and each other.

> How does the reality that thousands go to bed hungry each day impact the way you pray and live?

An Enlarged Sensitivity to Grace

To daily offer thanks for the gift and grace of bread on the table also nurtures an increased sensitivity to grace in all of its diverse forms.

For years, not fully understanding the nature and range of grace, I prayed for more grace for the tasks of specific days. Then one day I realized it was not a question of more grace, but a question of greater sensitivity to grace already present or to my ability to access grace.

In this context it is possible to define spiritual formation in terms of grace. A Christian is a person shaped by grace in order to become a source of grace to others.

> Research possible patterns of devotion and praying that might increase your sensitivity to grace.

> Describe your most profound experience at the Lord's Table.

An Enriched Skill in Accessing Grace

At Nazarene Theological Seminary students who participate in the basic course on spiritual formation are invited to identify the sources or means of grace that they use most efficiently. They also identify the means of grace that they fail to access with any regularity. Then they are asked to design a rule of life (with daily, weekly, monthly, quarterly, and annual patterns) by which they will seek to access grace more efficiently.

The syllabus invites them to design the rule of life with the aid of a small group of spiritual friends. They practice that rule of life for three months. With the help of a spiritual friend for correction and/or addition they re-aim their personal rule of life for the next quarter. The final report of the class is then submitted to the professors. The goal of the exercise is a visible and definable increase in the skill of accessing grace. It has been a personal joy to read these reports. Extending the practice of accessing grace from the daily request for bread at the table to the greater range of sources of grace creates a much richer spiritual formation.

> If you were to develop a "rule of life," where would you begin? What would be the primary elements?

A Growing Freedom from Materialism

In our affluent culture, consumerism and materialism have led to an extravagant use of daily bread. It is easy to depend upon things we can buy rather than on grace. This petition reminds us to trust God for our daily needs and not to extend the petition to include our daily wants.

> In your small group discuss ways you could counter the materialism of your culture.

A Growing Need to Share with the Less Fortunate

The longing to share bread and grace with others, combined with the recognition that everything we have comes from God, naturally leads us to become more gracious and giving people. Since we are only stewards of God's grace (a gift we never earned in the first place), we can dispense grace to all those around us without loss to ourselves. What a special joy to resource others through the grace God has granted to us so lavishly!

> During the next 30 days, participate in at least one intentional act of community compassion, and identify the effect upon your spiritual life.

The Connection Between Receiving and Thanksgiving

> What kind of healing will you seek the next time you go to the Lord's Table?

Just as there is a special connection between bread and God, a special connection lies between receiving and thanksgiving. People who try to hoard grace become miserly and ungrateful. People who learn to receive grace well become people who celebrate grace with thanksgiving.

People who have been blessed repeatedly sing praise to God. The music of praise flowing from a heart shaped by grace is exceptionally beautiful.

Implications for Participation in the Lord's Table

Although this fourth petition starts at the daily table of real bread, the fact that Jesus connected bread with the Last Supper alerts us to the abundance of grace available at the Lord's Table.

> Read Luke 24:13-32, and list three insights pertaining to the presence of Jesus at the breaking of the bread following His walk to Emmaus with the two disciples.

According to Luke 24, on that first Resurrection Day the disciples recognized Jesus while breaking bread. He continues to come to His disciples with massive amounts of grace at the Lord's Table.

A number of years ago after a dark, broken period of mid-life, as I harvested my personal spiritual journal I became aware of six or eight strategic moments at the Lord's Table. At each event, I was granted the grace of healing and rebuilding and renewal. I celebrate the grace of God in my life today because of the grace granted at His Table!

SIMPLE AND PROFOUND

This petition is basic and simple. At the same time, it's profound. To live and pray this prayer of total trust in God will reorient a person's life. People who pray this petition will become grace-sensitive, grace-filled, and grace-enabled grace dispensers.

May your life be shaped and formed by grace. May it begin at the Table!

SPIRITUAL FORMATION PRINCIPLE 12

Spiritual Formation Is Learning to Live
in the Physical and the Spiritual Worlds
at the Same Time.

8

"AND FORGIVE US OUR DEBTS, AS WE FORGIVE OUR DEBTORS" PART 1
FORGIVENESS—THE OUTRAGEOUS ACT THAT ADVANCES GOD'S GLOBAL WILL

D uring the 1990s Robert Enright, head of the department of educational psychology at the University of Wisconsin, Madison, offered well-attended seminars on forgiveness. In March 1995 he and Dr. Mack Harnden cosponsored a national conference on forgiveness, which I attended.

The second evening is forever burned into my mind. We watched the Public Broadcasting System documentary "From Fury to Forgiveness," which featured four people who had lost family members through vicious murders. The documentary followed each story from the murder to the murderer's identification, to the offer of forgiveness to the murderer.

After the film, three of its principals stepped on to the stage for questions. For the next two hours we discussed the dynamics of forgiveness—not just theories and principles, but the real-life impact of the gospel.

This petition for forgiveness brings us to the heart of the whole gospel. Lewis Smedes said, "Forgiving is the key to the entire Christian agenda."[1]

INSIGHTS FROM STRUCTURE

The structure of the Lord's Prayer again provides insight into the petition. In our V formation, this petition is opposite the complementary petition that God's will be done. In the complementary petition, the primary focus is upon God's saving will for the whole world. A major obstacle to the fulfillment of that saving will is the alienation created by sin. Forgiveness must become the hallmark of Christ's Body—and extend into the whole world.

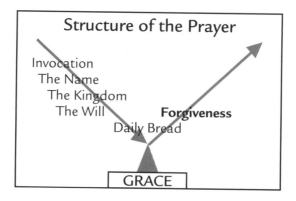

The ladder visualization of prayer underlines the sequence in another way. The person who rises each morning to lean his or her chin on the banister of heaven begins prayer with total focus upon God. The grand petitions of a holy name, a breaking-in kingdom, and a global saving will are followed by the request for daily bread. The petition for forgiveness moves deeper into the demands of daily living, into the search for reconciliation.

This prayer moves from understanding the divine design to the everyday needs of bread and forgiveness. It is impossible to be more practical and involved in daily activities.

When Jesus' disciples asked Him to teach them to pray (Luke 11), they were probably not prepared for the intensity of this prayer.

They were not expecting Him to die on a cross and offer forgiveness to those who executed Him. They had heard their Lord say, "If any want to become my followers, let them deny themselves and take up their cross and follow me" (Matt. 16:24), but they did not realize the extent of bearing that cross. They did not expect Him to offer them such a radical model.

When Reginald Denny, a truck driver

> In what specific ways do your praying and living identify you as a follower of Jesus?

> What is the relationship between forgiving and condoning? Between forgiving and tolerating?

beaten by police officers in Los Angeles, forgave his attackers, a reporter suggested he had suffered brain damage. From the world's point of view, forgiveness is outrageous.

INSIGHTS FROM THE TEXT

The first clue to this petition's importance is its involved nature in Greek. It is a double petition in which we request that God do something for us, and we promise to do something in return. The petition is much longer than all the other petitions by word count. The size and complexity of the petition point to its importance in the prayer.

"And" Points Toward the Connection of Bread and Forgiveness

The second grammatical indication in Greek of this petition's importance is the first appearance of the word "and" in the prayer. Our Lord chooses to tie the petition for bread closely to the petition for forgiveness.

SPIRITUAL FORMATION PRINCIPLE 13

Spiritual Formation Is Capturing the
Patterns of the Intangibles in Our Lives.

The only other appearance of "and" in the prayer ties the petition for forgiveness closely to the petition related to temptation. So the final three petitions have grammatical links.

The shift from asking for God's will to asking for our bread is surprising. It is even more surprising to move from asking for bread to asking for forgiveness. How are these two related?

> Recall a time when you forgave an undeserved hurt or betrayal. Describe what you thought, felt, and experienced.

Without the sustenance only God provides, our potential to do God's work is shattered. Without bread, we die.

Our need for forgiveness is equally straightforward. In our world, sin has alienated us from each other.

> If you were to take seriously the statement that "forgiveness is the difference between spiritual life and spiritual death," what difference would it make?

Without forgiveness we cannot find any solution to the sin problem. If the solution to sin is no longer available, the final result is spiritual death. Paul wrote, "The wages of sin is death, but the free gift of God is eternal life in Christ Jesus our Lord" (Rom.

6:23). Forgiveness—vertical and horizontal—is actually the difference between spiritual life and death.

Forgiveness and bread are also related in that they both are provided by God. The prayer for forgiveness and the prayer for bread are confessions of faith acknowledging our dependence on God.

The resistance to grace that flows from the sabotage of sin makes it more difficult to pray the Lord's Prayer with this dependence upon God. Humans have a phenomenal resistance to grace. The history of humanity is a battle between the rule of self and the rule of grace. Only the uncontaminated gift of God's grace in forgiveness can end that conflict.

OUR LORD'S TEACHING ON FORGIVENESS

The understanding of forgiveness was extended powerfully in our Lord's life, teachings, and model. The prediction that He would be Savior was clear in His ministry as a teacher. The model of His life underlines the depth and wisdom of His teachings.

The parable of the unforgiving servant in Matt. 18 is a fascinating illustration of Jesus' teachings. In the first of three acts, the king is settling accounts with his slaves. The first servant owes 10,000 talents (about 60,000,000 days' wages!) and cannot repay his debt. The king orders that he, his wife, his children, and all his possessions be sold to repay the debt. The servant begs the king to release him from his debt. Most graciously, the king does so.

In the second act, the first servant, who received such a gracious forgiveness, meets a fellow servant who owes him a debt of 100 days' wages. Contrary to the king's model of forgiveness, the first servant seizes the second servant and demands full repayment. The fellow servant pleads for mercy, but he is thrown into prison.

Classic justice occurs in the third act. The king learns of the unforgiving servant's misconduct. The authentic nature of forgiveness is emphasized by the king's rhetorical question: "Should you not have had mercy on your fellow slave as I had mercy on you?" (Matt. 18:33). The final verdict is that he must be tortured until the last coin is repaid.

> In your journal finish this sentence: When I read Matt. 18:33, I realize that I . . .

Forgiveness is a spectacular gift from the king. When forgiveness received does not result in forgiveness extended, a new kind of justice is imposed. When the mercy of forgiveness received becomes the measure of forgiveness extended, we are at the heart of our Lord's gospel.

The Spark in Jesus' Eye

I've often wished for a tape or video recording of Jesus' voice or face as He ended this parable. Listen carefully to the verse: "So my heavenly Father will also do to every one of you, if you do not forgive your brother or sister from your heart" (Matt. 18:35).

That verse holds a sense of final judgment—recognizing the vigorous resistance to grace and forgiveness aggravated by sin. Jesus must have also had a tear in His eye and voice, for He knew He would die to provide that forgiveness.

If we defined forgiveness in light of this parable alone, it would certainly include the forgiveness of all debts against us. The parable clearly teaches that forgiveness is available for the asking.

> In your journal finish this sentence: At this time in my spiritual life, forgiveness is . . .

"To be able to ask God the Father simply to remit debt and to overlook sins is *breathtaking*."[2] What a life-changing experience to be forgiven, set free by the loving Father in heaven!

> I attended a Promise Keepers Conference in 1995 with my two brothers. Late on Saturday afternoon, a young man my brother knew approached me: "I understand you are a minister." When I said I was, he asked, "What is forgiveness?"
>
> He told me about the vicious murder of his wife's brother by a drug-crazed "friend." Since the murderer's wife did not choose to care for their son, my questioner and his wife adopted the murderer's child to break the cycle of violence in that family.
>
> Tears welled in my eyes as I responded, "I know the technical and psychological and theological definitions of forgiveness. I have received forgiveness, and I have extended forgiveness to others. But I know of no person who has lived out Jesus' teachings and example as you and your wife are doing. You really live what you pray and pray what you live."

"TRESPASSES" OR "DEBTS" OR "SINS"?

A pastor who had led his congregation in praying the Lord's prayer for more than 30 years observed, "I've never quite understood why some people prefer to use 'trespasses' and others prefer to use 'debts.'"

Congregations often stumble over the choice of words when praying together. This detracts from the meaning and strength of the collective prayer.

Luke Prefers "Sins"

Evidently Matthew and Luke chose the different words to communicate more clearly to their specific audiences. Luke wrote to a law-oriented Roman audience, so his use of "sins" spoke decisively about the sin that divides us from our Heavenly Father and each other. Luke's choice underlines the legal significance of sin as an issue that fractures our relationship with God. We dare not trivialize sin to make forgiveness palatable.

Dallas Willard observes, "Today even many Christians read and say 'forgive us our trespasses' as 'give me a break.'"[3] The Greek word used here is often associated with synonyms that speak of refusal to keep the Law, and deliberate unrighteousness.

When Jesus directed us to pray for forgiveness of sins or trespasses, He was not trivializing sin. He was pointing directly to the heart of the gospel and to the genius of the Cross, the solution to the sin problem in the world.

Luke actually shifts from using "sins" in the first half of the petition to using "everyone indebted to us" in the second half of the phrase. Some commentators have suggested that this shift adds weight to the argument that Matthew's choice of "debts" is closer to the original Aramaic word Jesus actually used.

Matthew Prefers "Debts"

The importance of Matthew's use of "debts" is that it points beyond specific violations of the law (trespasses) and acknowledges the larger debt we owe to the Heavenly Father and those around us. The Hebrew word behind the Greek word in the Lord's Prayer points toward the inadequacies in our relationship with God. F. Hauck writes, "Later Judaism, which views the relation to God as a legal and business relation, often applies the metaphor of indebtedness to the ethical and legal relation between man and God. Man is in arrears with his good works and thus falls into debt with God."[4]

Matthew Uses "Trespasses" in Jesus' Next Comments

Although Matthew uses "debts" in the prayer, when Jesus comments on forgiveness in the subsequent verses, Matthew uses the verb "trespass." When William Tyndale translated the Bible into English in 1526, he mistranslated "debts" in the Lord's prayer as "trespasses." The *Book of Common Prayer* adopted Tyndale's version of the Lord's Prayer.[5] Today many congregations use "trespasses" in praying the Lord's Prayer in public.

The impossible debt we owe to God (whether we choose "debts" or "sins" or "trespasses") is strikingly illustrated in the parable of the wicked

servant (Matt. 18:23-35), in Luke 17's un-
profitable servant; and in the story of the
woman who was a great sinner (Luke 7:36-
50). The words alert us to the radical aware-
ness that we can never cancel the debt
through our own efforts.

> What are some ways
> you attempt to deal
> with sin when you do
> not want to forgive?

At the same time we are made aware that the guilt and trespasses and
obligations can be solved only in the context of forgiveness. And so we
address this petition to the only one who can bring a solution. Grace has
the final word—thanks be to God!

"Us" and "Our": We Never Pray Alone

The vigor of this petition is further extended when we observe the
plurals our Lord taught us to use in prayer. Sin, trespasses, guilt, and
debt are not just personal concerns but community issues. Matthew uses
five different grammatical pointers to emphasize the plural.

Our obligations to God, complicated by the sabotage of sin, are impossible apart from grace. We confess our dependence upon God's grace
whenever we repeat the Lord's Prayer. We can come as a community to
plead for the forgiveness that the Father so wonderfully offers.

The introduction of sin into the world created the need for forgiveness. Now Jesus teaches us that forgiveness is fully available and has become the hallmark of the Body of Christ. What a privilege to participate
in God's reconciling love and to offer it to others. We are indeed "ambassadors for Christ" (2 Cor. 5:20), and "we work together with him" (2 Cor.
6:1) in inviting others to know God's reconciling love through our Lord
Jesus Christ.

SPIRITUAL FORMATION PRINCIPLE 14

Spiritual Formation Is a
Journey Toward Wholeness.

Forgive Our Sins, as We Forgive

Rosamond E. Herklots

(Matt. 6:12-15; 18:21-35)

American Folk Hymn
Arr. by Lyndell Leatherman

1. "For - give our sins as we____ for - give," You
2. How can Your par - don reach____ and ____ bless the
3. In blaz - ing light Your Cross____ re - veals the
4. Lord, cleanse the depths with - in____ our ____ souls and

taught us, Lord, to pray. But You a - lone can
un - for - giv - ing heart That broods on____ wrongs and
truth we dim - ly knew, How small the____ debts men
bid re - sent - ment cease. Then, rec - on - ciled to

grant____ us____ grace to____ live the words we____ say.
will____ not____ let old____ bit - ter - ness de - part?
owe____ to____ us, how____ great our debt to____ You!
God ____ and man, our____ lives will spread Your peace.

9

"AND FORGIVE US OUR DEBTS, AS WE FORGIVE OUR DEBTORS" PART 2
FORGIVENESS—RESPONDING TO THE INJUSTICES OF LIFE

He was raised in a home scarred by an emotionally disturbed father. After his mother's death, the father put the boys up for adoption.

In a class on spiritual formation, the young man began to deal with the traumas of his life by writing a conversation with Jesus in his journal. He asked the Lord, "What am I going to do about my father and the damage he imposed on me?"

The Lord responded, "You will have to forgive him. If you fail to forgive, you may inflict similar damage upon your children."

Great sobs began to wrack his whole body. Then he looked up through his tears and said, "I forgive you, Daddy. I love you, Daddy." What a profound moment!

At the next class session, he observed, "The most dramatic change occurred when I realized that when I forgave my father, I also forgave God."[1]

In this man's mind and heart, he had blamed God for letting his father create such a dysfunctional home. Through the double forgiveness, his relationship with both his earthly father and his Heavenly Father changed in an instant.

A FUNDAMENTAL PRINCIPLE IN SPIRITUAL FORMATION

> How would you define the "messes" of life?

In forgiving his earthly father, my friend learned one of the fundamental principles of spiritual formation: One of the more rapid routes to spiritual growth is to give God the greatest messes in your life. These messes nearly always involve forgiveness—and forgiveness is essential to community.

The previous chapter focused on the primary biblical and theological clues to the meaning of this petition. Two issues require further attention—the emphasis upon community and the significance of structure.

Forgiveness is the quintessential Christian act . . . the hardest chord to play in the human repertoire.
—Lewis Smedes

Community: Personal, But Never Private

The petition for daily bread is also set firmly within the context of community. Jesus, in teaching His disciples how to pray, places all of us into the heart of community. The disciples-apprentices of our Lord are pledged to Him exclusively. The commitment to the Kingdom calls for full allegiance. There are personal issues but never private issues. The personal issues are always subordinate to the demands of the community.

> ### SPIRITUAL FORMATION PRINCIPLE 15
> Spiritual Formation Is Both
> Corporate and Personal—Never Private.

Individual disciples of our Lord now think and live and pray and function in community. Our time, our money, our attitudes, our investments, our service, our very being is at the King's disposal. At no point is the role of community more critical than in the issue of forgiveness.

We pray for bread in community and thereby acknowledge our dependence upon God as the source of all we have and are. Now we

> What areas of your life need the healing restoring grace of God?

> In your small group or Sunday School Class, discuss ways you could facilitate forgiveness and reconciliation where you live and work.

> How could an appropriate support group facilitate healing and wholeness in your life just now?

are urged to pray for forgiveness in community, acknowledging that the miracle of forgiveness can flow only from the equally magnificent miracle of God's grace at Calvary. We are never more like our Lord than when we are receiving or extending forgiveness.

INSIGHT FROM THE COMPLEMENTARY PETITION

The literary structure of the Lord's Prayer shows the connection between the petition for forgiveness and its complementary petition of asking God to accomplish His transforming will in our broken world.

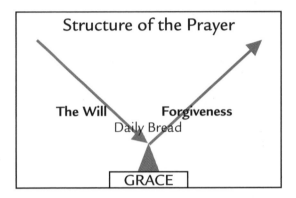

We have already discussed "Thy Will Be Done" as a focus upon God's saving and transforming will. The first three petitions are parallel in the sense that they focus upon God's grand design for the whole world. In each case, however, the petition does have a personal side in which the petitioner

> In what ways could you be an agent of forgiveness for someone else today?

offers to submit to that grand global transformation and pleads for the privilege of participating in it.

When we look at the broken people in the world, we see that the longing for reconciliation requires forgiveness. Paul recognizes the essence of the petition for God's will to be done: "All this is from God, who reconciled us to himself through Christ, and has given us the ministry of reconciliation" (2 Cor. 5:18).

As the Lord's Prayer moves from God's grand design to the application of those petitions on an earthly plane, forgiveness takes center stage. As alienated, sinful humans are reconciled to God through the grace of forgiving love, God's will is dramatically accomplished.

As that forgiveness moves from the reconciliation between God and humans to reconciliation between humans, we see the grand transformation of God's will. That leads Paul to declare: "Yes, everything is for your sake, so that grace, as it extends to more and more people, may increase thanksgiving, to the glory of God" (2 Cor. 4:15).

The Danger of Lying As We Pray

The petition for forgiveness is different from previous petitions in length and grammatical structure. It is also different in having an apparent condition attached to it: "Forgive as we forgive." If the second half of the petition is taken as a precondition to the first, forgiveness suddenly becomes virtually unattainable. From a theological point of view, it becomes a works righteousness, by which we earn God's favor—contrary to the doctrine of grace.

> H. A. Williams in *Tensions* pointed out that if we yell over the banister of heaven and demand justice, we will certainly receive exact justice. If we plead for grace, we will receive abundant and amazing grace.

Paul's discussion of reconciliation in 2 Corinthians clarifies that God's forgiveness always precedes our forgiveness. God initiates the process through the Atonement. He extends the process by inviting us to become His ambassadors who spread forgiveness.

So why is the second half of the petition included in the prayer? The parable of the ungrateful servant in Matt. 18 provides the answer. The person who receives God's amazing grace of forgiveness is now forever indebted to God. Accepting that loving forgiveness obligates us to extend forgiveness to others as well.

Suddenly this petition becomes a double-edged sword. The credibility of our praying and living are clearly called into judgment. If we beg God for forgiveness and refuse to forgive others, we are praying a lie (or we are lying as we pray).[2] If we, like the ungrateful servant, refuse to forgive those indebted to us, the other side of grace

> In what areas of your life are you close to inviting God to dispense justice rather than grace?

becomes visible. The judgment that has been suspended is reversed. Total justice is demanded. Every debt becomes due. This two-member petition underlines the essence of God's grace.

To pray this petition is a pledge to forgive others—to participate in redeeming relationships in our broken world.

THE IMPLICATIONS FOR SPIRITUAL FORMATION

This petition's substantial implications for spiritual formation deserve careful attention. Paul observes that "all have sinned and fall short of the glory of God" (Rom. 3:23). His personification of sin as a beast that deceives and alienates and kills is written in vivid language in Romans. The only adequate solution to the problem of sin is found in the atonement purchased for us at the Cross.

The injustices of life frequently grow out of the sabotage of sin. We can often skillfully disguise the damage and limp along on the side roads of spiritual formation.

Whether those injustices are self-inflicted or inflicted upon us, we need the power of forgiveness to step into the greatest opportunities for spiritual formation.

1. The End of Denial

The first step in responding to life's injustices is to stop disguising the damage. We must acknowledge that sin has invaded our lives and crippled our spiritual formation.

The longer we deny that we have been damaged, the more difficult we find it to open ourselves to others and to God's grace.

During the Desert Storm military campaign in the Persian Gulf area, the commander of operations would appear on newscasts and say, "The bomb damage assessment is not yet available." Many people short-circuit the potential of healing grace by refusing to acknowledge or assess the levels of damage that have occurred in their lives.

2. Ownership of Response

The second step is to stop blaming others for the pain inflicted upon us. Others do impose much of the mutilation upon us. We are deceived and seduced by people already caught in the webs of sin. Such people try to assuage their own guilt by dragging others into the quagmire of sin.

Sometimes people we have trusted inflict damage. I will never forget the testimony of a young man who said, "I recall walking into a snowstorm during junior high. My best friend had just betrayed me, and I vowed I would never let anyone ever get close enough to me to betray me again. I have kept that promise. But today, for me, God is barely warm, and I have become a semi-mobile corpse." The betrayal had created an accumulating level of damage in his life.

When we stop blaming the friend, colleague, parent, sibling, or stranger who inflicted damage, we surrender the right to get even. We begin to survey our damage and search for the healing God has so graciously provided. We begin to own our own pain and bring it to the only source of healing—God himself.

3. Forgiveness

As I reflected on this process and tried to identify the steps in responding to injustice, I showed my initial list to a close spiritual friend. She was startled that I included forgiveness so early in the list. I suspect one of the most deceitful evidences of sin is the desire to delay forgiveness.

In 1985 Ronald Reagan, then president of the United States, offered to place a wreath at the Tomb of the Unknown Soldier in Bitburg, West Germany. People from all over the world were incensed, thinking, *It's only been 40 years. It's too early to forgive.*

As our Lord taught us, it's never too early to forgive. First, we need to realize that forgiveness and reconciliation are not synonymous. It requires only one person (enabled by God's grace) to offer forgiveness. It requires two people (the one who offers and the one who receives) to achieve reconciliation. However, if the recipient does not respond, the offer of forgiveness is not invalidated.

Second, we need to remember that forgiveness does not automatically erase the scars of the original hurt. The scar may ache again, but never with the original energy and the memory of that hurt has been changed.

> Make a list of people to whom you need to extend forgiveness—whether or not reconciliation occurs. What are the first steps you will take?

Third, forgiveness does not condone the act. Forgiving child abuse or adultery is not admitting that such acts are permissible. It means, in Thielicke's terms, that the bond of relationship is too great to sacrifice it to this act.[3]

4. Release the Mess to God

Once the wonderful graciousness of forgiveness has entered the scene, it's much easier to release the whole mess to God and let Him work it out. Forgiveness teaches us that we cannot find the solution ourselves—we rest in grace.

5. Future Strategy

The fifth step is to move from the paralysis of the trauma to live into the future. Once we have released the whole mess into God's care, we can step into God's new day for us.

Future strategy calls for specific steps by which we move away from the shadow of the pain and live freely and wisely under God.

6. Learn to Trust Again

An inevitable result of sin's sabotage is difficulty trusting others. When trust is betrayed, we become wary of trusting others.

Only after forgiveness has begun to solve the issue can we begin trusting again. The process may be slow, but it's crucial to a healthy relationship with God and others.

Since the end of the war I had a home in Holland for victims of Nazi brutality. Those who were able to forgive their former enemies were able also to return to the outside world and rebuild their lives, no matter what the physical scars. Those who nursed their bitterness remained invalids. It was as simple and horrible as that.
—Corrie ten Boom

7. Forgive Yourself

One damage that sin inflicts is the tendency to blame ourselves inappropriately. That blame often moves into a deep shame. If God can forgive us, we should forgive ourselves. Then we can accept ourselves for what we are. We must keep that distinction very clear. Learning to forgive yourself may be even more difficult than trusting others again.

8. Forgive God

At first glance the idea of forgiving God seems preposterous. Who are we to think we have the right to forgive God?

When we have suffered from an injustice, we often blame God for failing to solve the issue directly. When we acknowledge our sense of betrayal by God, we are in position to ask for forgiveness for that attitude. It's amazing how much freedom results from forgiving God.

> In your journal tell how you would implement each of the eight steps. Write a paragraph or letter to God about each one.

The gospel offers us such good news! Life's "messes" are not the last word. Forgiveness lets us be released from the chains of the past and walk into the future under grace. Thanks be to God!

10

"AND LEAD US NOT INTO TEMPTATION"
THE KINGDOM REVERSES THE RAVAGES OF SIN

A t the end of our visit, it was apparent that my Uncle Chris did not want us to leave. Finally he blurted to my mother, "Pauline, I've never known the intensity of temptation I've encountered in these last months."

My mother, prompted, I'm certain, by the Holy Spirit, looked into her dear brother's face and said, "Well, praise the Lord. If the evil one had you under his control, it wouldn't be necessary to apply such great pressure to you!"

The relief that flashed across my uncle's face was marvelous. It's startling to recognize that three of the Gospels report the terrifying intensity of temptation that our Lord encountered. How could 40 days and nights of temptation be condensed into such a vivid story?

> Read Matt. 4:1-11. Using your God-given imagination, picture yourself in the scene. Describe the sounds, smells, and your feelings.

> Describe the last time you faced temptation. What did you do about it?

INSIGHTS FROM STRUCTURE

The structure of the Lord's Prayer we have been using focuses on the balance between the petition for the Kingdom to come and the complementary petition for freedom from temptation. In the petition for the Kingdom to come, the focus lies on the blessings of this new Kingdom inaugurated by our Lord. The astonishing truth of the Kingdom is that those blessings that many generations thought would come only in some far, distant future have suddenly appeared in Jesus.

In this complementary petition, Jesus recommends that we pray that

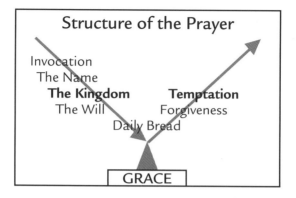

we would not be led into temptation. We recognize that the sabotage of sin is sinister and powerful. We acknowledge that membership in the Kingdom does not bring any immunity from opposition. We're aware that deliverance can come only from the King himself.

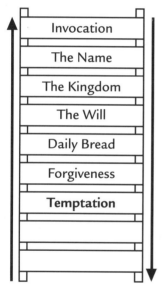

When we think of the prayer in terms of the ladder metaphor, the prayer takes on added meaning. Each morning we arise and begin by seeking God, His name, His kingdom, and His will. The daily bread enables us to join reconciliation through forgiveness. Now Jesus instructs us to connect the escape from temptation to the petition for forgiveness and bread.

We have moved from the profundity of the heavenly scene to the depths of pain created by sin. What a profound prayer!

INSIGHTS FROM THE TEXT

Only twice does the conjunction "and" appear in the Lord's Prayer. The first time, it signals the essential connection between bread and forgiveness. Apart from physical bread, we die physically; and apart from forgiveness, we die emotionally and spiritually. Now our Lord binds the petition for deliverance from temptation directly to the two earlier petitions.

> In your journal, write to the Lord and ask Him where you might be dying emotionally and spiritually from unforgiveness.

Joining the Kingdom of God places us in a context in which the opposition to Jesus and the Kingdom dramatically impacts our lives. The battle between God and His opposition threatens to destroy us. Our only hope is an implicit faith in God.

Small wonder that Paul used the military language of "the whole armor of God" to talk about this engagement. Paul and our Lord tell us that this battle is fierce and demanding. It can never be won in our own strength. It's the picture of God's people on a journey, picking their way through a field of deadly obstacles and traps. But we're assured that God's armor is sufficient.

"Temptation"—to Entice or to Test?

The most critical word in this petition is "temptation." Thinking through issues surrounding temptation forces us to understand God and ourselves more precisely. Fuzzy theology will never help us grasp this critical issue of daily living in a sinful world.

There are so many references to temptation and testing in the Bible that Ernst Lohmeyer suggested the Bible could be called "the Book of Temptations." "On its first pages stands the temptation of the first man and woman, and on its last the prophetic descriptions of the great temptation which is 'coming on the whole world, to try those who dwell on the earth' (Rev. 3.10)."

—Ernst Lohmeyer
"Our Father," An Introduction to the Lord's Prayer, 25

Martin Luther suffered terrible temptations. The enemy was so real to him that he was reported to have hurled his inkwell at him. Luther's expositions on the Lord's Prayer tend to understand temptation from the viewpoint of threat and seduction. When we look at the different Bible passages that use the language of temptation, it's fairly easy to organize them into four categories:

1. Humans test God.
2. God tests humans.
3. Other people tempt us.
4. Satan tempts us.

These categories are subcategories of the two basic meanings of temptation: testing to demonstrate authenticity, and seduction to destroy and pervert.

TEMPTATION AS TESTING

A. Humans Test God.

The classic example of humans testing God in the Old Testament is the Exodus story. The Israelites forever grumbled against God. For instance, Exod. 17 tells of people quarrelling because of the lack of water. Moses asks, "Why do you quarrel with me? Why do you test the LORD?" (v. 2).

The story of Ananias and Sapphira from Acts also fits this category. They attempted to play games with God and the young church by pretending to give the whole price of their land to the church. Peter asked, "How is it that you have agreed together to put the Spirit of the Lord to the test?" (Acts 5:9). Ananias and Sapphira discovered "It is a fearful thing to fall into the hands of the living God" (Heb. 10:31).

B. God Tests Humans.

In numerous biblical examples, God tests people to demonstrate their integrity, such as Abram's bitter test in Gen. 22. God asks Abram to offer his only son, the son of promise, to Him. Only at the last moment does God intervene.

Job responds to his wife with the fundamental question of those caught in the storm of testing, "Shall we receive the good at the hand of God, and not receive the bad?" (Job 2:10). Several New Testament passages reflect the same understanding of testing. For example, Paul declares, "No testing has overtaken you that is not common to everyone. God is faithful, and he will not let you be tested beyond your strength, but with the testing he will also provide the way out so that you may be able to endure it" (1 Cor. 10:12-13; see also 1 Pet. 1:6-7 and James 1:2-4).

> Describe a time when you were tested by God. How did you grow from it?

In each of these cases the testing is not to destroy, but for discipline, maturation, and perfection in integrity. The good news is that God will limit the testing.

TEMPTATION AS ENTICEMENT OR SEDUCTION

A. Other People Tempt Us.

The Bible honestly reveals the wide range of deceit, seduction, trickery, sham, and pretense in our broken world. There appears to be a community in sin as well, for people often attempt to drag others into their degradation, as the vivid descriptions of sin in Rom. 1 reflect.

> How have you been deceived or enticed into temptation by others? How did you handle it?

The goal of this kind of enticement is to destroy and pervert. Recognizing that evil is not simply personal but also systemic alerts us to the wide range of manipulative temptations in society. Temptations, masquerading as freedoms, are merchandised in a wide array of colors. They are like an undetected cancer that eats away at the very fiber of our spiritual lives.

B. Satan Tempts Us.

The Book of Job lets us listen as Satan requests the privilege of tempting Job. Within boundaries God has designed, Satan is permitted to attempt to seduce Job.

Jesus' temptation is also a dramatic picture of the devil's offering Jesus shortcuts to the objectives of the Messiah. Satan obviously sought to trap Jesus into a pseudo-success that would betray His trust in God.

> In what ways have you been enticed to take inappropriate shortcuts?

New Testament passages describing the final days show testing at its ultimate intensity. When we enter the colorful chambers of the Book of Revelation, we see that the sinister work of the evil one lurks behind every corner in a battle to the finish against God. Many are maimed in the battle—even though we know the victory at the Cross guarantees final success.

With my farm background I have come to appreciate the end-times analogy to a chicken being butchered. When the chicken's head is removed, its gyrations cover everyone in the vicinity with blood. Likewise, although Satan's final fate has already been sealed at the Cross, the final bloody gyrations will affect us. Recognizing the intensity of the battle, we're taught to pray for escape from temptation—whether it's testing or enticement.

The petition for escape from temptation covers both testing for approval of quality and seduction that leads to destruction. The fundamental issue is a trust in God that counters the final destructive force of testing.

"Us"—Never Alone in Temptation

With the use of "us," Jesus again points toward the power of commu-

> In what area have you been trying to win the battle against temptation in your own strength?

nity. Temptation is real, and we need help. If we were contending against only flesh and blood, it might be simpler. But we don't stand a chance against the principalities and powers, apart from a delivering God and a supportive community.

"NOT": THE NEGATIVE OF HUMBLE DEPENDENCE

In this petition we meet the first and only negative, in the Lord's Prayer. To pray "Lead us into temptation" (without the negative) would be a move toward some kind of personal heroism—some grand exam in which we could prove our own mettle, integrity, and victory.

> In your journal, describe a time when temptation caused you to draw closer to God.

The negative, however, introduces a totally different picture. We dare not provoke the conflict, for it is far too subtle for us to handle alone.

By teaching us to use the negative, Jesus invited us to express a humble trust in God. In it, the community confesses reliance upon God at every juncture of testing.

"LEAD"—REMEMBERING THAT GOD NEVER SEDUCES

What does it mean to ask God not to lead us into temptation? If God is leading us into the temptation that may destroy us, what does that say about His character?

James was already thinking about this when he wrote, "No one, when tempted, should say, 'I am being tempted by God'; for God cannot be tempted by evil and he himself tempts no one" (1:13).

So what did Jesus intend when He instructed His disciples to pray this petition? Jesus knew that God is not an abusive ogre who would lead us into a potentially deadly trap.

> What weapons do you use to fight temptation? List them in order of your favorite or best weapon. What weapons does God offer that you're not currently using?

In Matt. 24:22 Jesus acknowledges that the intensity of the final evil could be overwhelming, but God, in His wisdom and love, will limit the testing to protect His people. The request that God not lead us into temptation includes a plea for Him to intervene on our behalf.

We *do* dare to throw ourselves totally on God's mercy with our elder brother, Jesus.

He has faced temptation for us as our great High Priest, "For we do not have a high priest who is unable to sympathize with our weaknesses, but we have one who in every respect has been tested as we are, yet without sin. Let us therefore approach the throne of grace with boldness, so that we may receive mercy and find grace to help in time of need" (Heb. 4:15-16).

In the final analysis, this petition is a confession of total trust in the God who alone can deliver His community in Christ. We need Him to deliver us when we get caught in the undertow of evil.

IMPLICATIONS FOR SPIRITUAL FORMATION

If you and I could pray and live this petition, what kind of spiritual formation would develop?

1. Spiritual formation would grow from a totally God-dependent relationship. The nature of the treacherous testing would keep us very close to God.

2. We would find no room for arrogance or self-sufficiency that would lead to temptations. The clear knowledge that personal resources cannot solve the problems of evil would lead to a life shaped by grace.

SPIRITUAL FORMATION PRINCIPLE 16

Spiritual Formation Is Reflected in Personal Lifestyle and Exhibited in Redemptive Action in Our World.

---

3. The knowledge that "because he himself was tested by what he suffered, he is able to help those who are being tested" (Heb. 2:18) provides a base from which we can operate. We are never alone in this struggle, because our Lord, the great High Priest, has been there ahead of us.

4. People who live such a grace-filled life close to the Master learn to live in community. That community is never more unified than when it faces opposition together. Wes Tracy wrote, "The wisdom of 20 Christian centuries raises itself on one elbow and in a tone that tells us we should need no reminder, informs us that none of us can long stay on the path of the holy life if we travel alone."[1]

> Covenant with God to find a trusted Christian friend to hold you accountable. Begin praying now for the Holy Spirit to help find such a person.

Knowing the true terrors of being separated from God through temptation, we dare pray, "Lead us not into temptation." Knowing the true nature of the God, who promises to deliver, we are not overcome when testing comes. We have a Gethsemane-tested faith in a God who cares. Knowing ourselves through the Golgotha mirror, we can place ourselves securely in the keeping of a resurrected Savior. That may be the greatest practical theology of all time.

11

"BUT DELIVER US FROM EVIL"
THE DRAMATIC RESCUE THAT HALLOWS GOD'S NAME

*T*he overpowering weight of evil was palpably present and crushed my chest to the point I had difficulty breathing. I was walking through the underground Yad Vashem "museum" built to commemorate the Holocaust in Jerusalem. The pictures and artifacts were stunning. People spoke only in whispers. The sheer magnitude of the evil that led to the wholesale slaughter of so many millions of Jews was staggering. When we exited, the bright light of day was nearly too much to bear. I found it difficult to sleep that night —and many nights since. What kind of a world do we live in? What does it mean to pray "but deliver us from evil" in a context like this?

> In your group, list the evidences of the increase of evil in our culture. How can, or how should, we respond as a community of faith?

INSIGHTS FROM STRUCTURE

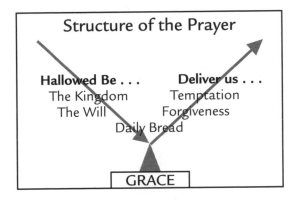

Structure of the Prayer

Hallowed Be . . .
The Kingdom
The Will

Deliver us . . .
Temptation
Forgiveness

Daily Bread

GRACE

The first three petitions emphasize submissive obedience to God's great design. The three final petitions focus upon implicit trust in God. The petition for daily bread points directly to the life of grace—toward the radical optimism of grace that gives perspective and hope in our broken world.

The complementary petition is for God to hallow His name. The petition for deliverance is a request for the divine nick-of-time rescue from the totally impossible situation as a vivid demonstration of God's holiness at work. The rescue will be so dramatic that every observer will acknowledge that the only explanation is the intervention of a Holy God.

INSIGHTS FROM THE SEQUENCE

As we descend farther down the ladder, we start the crucial work of becoming forgiven people who spread forgiveness. When testing turns into an alluring temptation, we stand confidently in God's full armor (Eph. 6). Even when we have been forced to a standstill, we can wait in the strength God provides.

In this final petition, "but deliver us from evil," we acknowledge that sin is too great an enemy to conquer on our own. We depend on the energetic grace of divine deliverance conclusively demonstrated at the Cross.

INSIGHTS FROM THE TEXT

The presence of the conjunction "but" has often been used as evidence that the sixth and seventh petitions should be viewed as one. On the other hand, the conjunction points to the idea of dramatic deliverance.

The conjunction clarifies the meaning of the sixth petition. "Lead us not into temptation" expresses a longing for escape from the testing or seductive aspects of our world. The conjunction admits that the ideal of no testing is impossible in a world contaminated by sin.

To recognize that we can't escape from temptation does not mean we resign ourselves to failure. "But" declares that God has an "escape from temptation" beyond anything the tempter has ever devised.

"Deliver"—the power of the verb

The Greek word for "deliver" is rare in the New Testament, but it is decisive. Its primary meaning is "to draw out of danger by drawing to oneself." The tense of the Greek verb suggests terms such as "extricate" and "snatch from danger." The light of hope shines in it.

When our Lord was on the Cross, His torturers sneered, "Let God deliver him now." Only a divine intervention could save Him (Matt. 27:43). The triple use of the word in 2 Cor. 1:9-10 shows us that Paul's persecution was so extreme he was certain he would not survive. "Indeed, we felt that we had received the sentence of death so that we would rely not on ourselves but on God who raises the dead. He who *rescued* us from so deadly a peril will continue to *rescue* us; on him we have set our hope that he will *rescue* us again" (emphasis added). The extrication is so dramatic because it arrives when all other hope has been extinguished.

> Describe in your journal a time when you were "extricated." What happened? How did you feel? How did God deliver you?

Its energy is heightened when we reflect on the power of temptation in the final contest with evil in the end time. Peter echoes the Lord's Prayer when he writes, "The Lord knows how to rescue the godly from trial, and to keep the unrighteous under punishment until the day of judgment" (2 Pet. 2:9).

"The evil"—or "the evil one"

In expounding this petition, the hardest grammatical problem has been choosing "the evil" or "the evil one." Greek grammar permits either choice.

The larger biblical context does not force a choice either. The Old Testament references to evil are easily sorted into three major classifications: evil people from whom we need deliverance, evil circumstances from which we need deliverance, and evil inclinations of our own hearts.

The New Testament uses neuter forms of this adjective that obviously refer to evil in general. With these neuter references are masculine references to Satan as "the evil one." Behind the great threat of evil lies the sinister conspirator who seeks to alienate people from God. So the neuter and masculine interpretations are related to each other in the New Testament.

The danger to the true followers of our Lord cannot be overstated. Jesus prays for the protection of His followers in John 17:15—"I am not asking you to take them out of the world, but I ask you to protect them from the evil one." We need divine help to resist this inveterate enemy of God. That is the heart of this petition.

Satan's final overthrow is decisively announced. Paul says in Col. 2:15, "[Christ] disarmed the rulers and authorities and made a public example of them, triumphing over them in it." Jesus pronounced Satan's final defeat in Matt. 25:41—"Then he will say to those at his left hand, 'You that are accursed, depart from me into the eternal fire prepared for the devil and his angels.'"

I agree with Karl Barth in his discussion of the Lord's Prayer: "Ask me no questions about the Demon, for I am not an authority on the subject! However, it is necessary for us to know that the Devil exists, but then we must hasten to get away from him."[1] We are challenged to think first of God's gracious work in salvation—and only then to think about the application of the atonement to the problems of sin and evil.

Thus, our Lord teaches us to respond to the evil in our world. Through God's grace, the power of the atonement, and the accountability of community, we find ultimate freedom.

LESSONS FROM JESUS' DELIVERANCE FROM TEMPTATION

We find great comfort in the fact that our Lord faced intense temptations. They centered on two fundamental issues: The quality of His relationship with the Father and the methods by which He would accomplish His messianic goals.

Our Lord's responses offer hope for us in our own testing.

Jesus implicitly trusted God's revealed word and chose to be obedient to it. Total trust and obedience in the word forms the foundation to resolve temptation.

> How does the experience of Jesus in the Garden make a difference in our encounters with temptation?

Our Lord's trust in the Father did not require proof before obedience. The first two temptations are preceded by "If you are the Son of God." Satan invited Jesus to demonstrate His relationship to the Father through miracles. In the third temptation, Satan invited Him to select a shortcut to spiritual dominion. But our Lord trusted without demanding proof.

> Describe a time when you "learned obedience" through temptation.

The wilderness temptation was child's play compared to Jesus' testing in the Garden of Gethsemane. This testing was so intense that Jesus sweat drops of blood. The obedience "learned" through His lifetime ends in the grand victory that purchases our salvation. So Jesus is not simply a wonderful model of facing temptation—He is the one who took our place and paid our penalty.

The Cross provides the answer to this seventh petition, "Deliver us."

What happened at the Cross means sin does not have the final word. Thanks be to God!

IMPLICATIONS FOR SPIRITUAL FORMATION

Trusting in a God who specializes in deliverance totally reorients life.

Ability to Face Evil Realistically

I'm amazed by the popularity of novels dealing with the rapture and related topics. It's not necessary to trivialize evil as so many popular writers do. We can recognize evil for all that it is. At the same time, it's not wise to overemphasize and give undue publicity to evil. The biblical injunction is for soberness, alertness, and implicit trust in the God who specializes in deliverance.

The Security of Trusting in a Delivering God

Some years ago I read of ingenious attempts to protect skyscrapers from earthquakes. The primary damage from earthquakes comes when the building sways beyond design limitations and threatens to develop harmonic rhythms that will result in disintegration.

One solution captured my imagination. In New York's Citicorp skyscraper, officials placed a 210-ton block of concrete on hy-

> Write a personal spiritual autobiography about the time when God's grace delivered you from temptation. How did those experiences contribute to your spiritual growth?

The class assignment was to come up with five "landmarks" (positive pivotal moments) and five "landmines" (negative pivotal moments) in our lives. The landmines were easy, but the landmarks were harder: what had God really ever done for me? I could come up with only four landmarks.

When I plotted them on the timeline of my life, I saw all of my landmines happened in my 13th year: deaths among friends and family, my father's desertion. The realization hit me like a truck: *This year has controlled my whole life!* I had never forgiven, and so had lived with the evil of that one year for almost 15 years. I cried out to God, *O Father, please give me the grace to forgive. Please free me from this!*

At that point I knew this petition, "deliver us from evil," was not only a request to prevent evil, as I had thought all my life. This deliverance can also be *cure.* As the Son began to shine upon my personal history, I recognized that this was my fifth landmark. God had indeed done something powerful for me.

—a student in the Spiritual Formation Module at Nazarene Theological Seminary

draulic stabilizers on the 88th floor of the building. When the building exceeds the normal sway of 6 to 7 feet, the computer actuates the hydraulics to move the concrete block in the opposite direction. This dampens the effects of the sway and saves the building.

> Identify your support team or accountability partners. If you don't have a support team, how will you find one?

God's love in a believer's heart becomes the counterweight to the destructive blows of life. We're rescued repeatedly from what appears to be a certain death sentence.

Living Within a Delivered Community

> Describe a time when accountability protected you—or could have if you had been open to it.

We are free to live wisely within the Body of Christ. The accountability and reinforcement of the community protects us. The success of 12-step programs demonstrates the power of community. May the Church become such a force of deliverance and stability.

Protection from End-Time Speculators

The security and stability of living as we pray and praying as we live protects us from wild speculations of people who go overboard on end-time themes. Those who exaggerate the cultic and the apocalyptic lose their theological balance and create problems for themselves and for the Church.

Paul showed that the whole armor of God is offensive rather than defensive. He also reminds us that the proclamation of salvation takes precedence over end-time speculation.

Praying Facing God—Rather than Facing Problems

Our Lord taught us to pray this prayer with a designated structure. To reverse that direction leads to imbalance and emphasis upon minor issues.

People who begin praying from the standpoint of their own needs become obsessed with their own demands. They attempt to manipulate God and others to meet their own perception.

People who follow the Lord's Prayer as our Lord taught us will climb the ladder of prayer and fill their minds, heart, and emotions with God and His grand design. Problems will recede to their appropriate size and will be seen in light of the God who delivers. What a difference in perspective!

Jesus invited us to pray in a way that our vision of God and His call to

holiness and purity will fill us. The grander vision of the call to relationship and the comfort of the divine presence will be the first step toward
our longed-for deliverance.

Frederick Dale Bruner paraphrased this seventh petition as follows:
"Dear Father, please lead us in such a way that we will be able to resist the
temptations that both consciously and unconsciously surround us;
please constantly swoop down and rescue us from all the wiles of the evil
one and all his evil works—we need your help."[2]

*Now that's living the Lord's Prayer! That's total trust in the God who alone can
deliver!*

SPIRITUAL FORMATION PRINCIPLE 17

Spiritual Formation Is Healing Through
Daring to Identify and Face Fears, Anxieties,
Scars, and Memories Through the
Enabling Power of the Holy Spirit.

Father, Your Name

Based on Matthew 6:9-10

Fa-ther, Your name, Your King-dom, Your will____ Here on earth as it is in heav - en. Fa-ther, Your name, Your King-dom, Your will____ Here on earth as it is in heav - en. For Yours is the pow-er And Yours all the glo-ry For - ev - er - more.____ A - men. For Yours is the pow-er And Yours all the glo-ry For - ev - er - more.__ A - men.

WORDS & MUSIC: Ken Bible

FATHER, YOUR NAME
Irregular

12

"FOR THINE IS THE KINGDOM, AND THE POWER, AND THE GLORY, FOR EVER. AMEN"
THE PERSPECTIVE OF PRAISE THAT FLOWS FROM A RELATIONSHIP WITH THE FATHER

As I watched Princess Diana's funeral on television in September 1997, the worship leader invited the congregation to pray the Lord's Prayer in their own languages. The hair on the back of my neck stood as I realized that more people were probably praying the Lord's Prayer in more languages at the same time than ever before in history. I really believe that the center of gravity in the whole universe shifted that morning.

> In your journal write a prayer in which you end with a deliberate pronouncement of praise and glory to God.

> In your small group, share significant experiences of praying the Lord's Prayer in public.

I could only celebrate and worship the Father to whom we were praying.

It is also an extraordinary moment when a congregation ends the Lord's Prayer and announces its trust in God's promises revealed in the prayer. Who can measure the results of such prayers?

Is the Doxology Original?

There has been a great deal of confusion over the origin of the doxology, because modern English versions place the doxology in a footnote indicating that the earliest manuscripts don't contain these words. The doxology does appear in the Didache—a very early summary of Christian teaching. The doxology quoted there reads, "for yours is the power, and the glory." The word "kingdom" is absent, and the final "Amen" is not quoted.

The words of this doxology are present in David's prayer when he asked God to guide Solomon in building the temple in 1 Chron. 29:10-11, 13. The Lord's Prayer is the biblical text most frequently discussed by ancient Christian writers. Most later biblical manuscripts witness to the universal usage of this wonderful benediction acknowledging God as the ultimate source of all things.

> In your small group, describe what it would mean for your congregation to "break into grand flurries of praise and adoration."

The benediction captures the flavor not only of the prayer but of our Master, who taught us to pray this way. Worshiping people naturally break into grand flurries of praise and adoration.

INSIGHTS FROM STRUCTURE

The invocation sets the stage for praying to the Father, who is the Creator and the Redeemer. Now in the final complementary phrase of the prayer, the worshiper praises the one who has made this possible. The doxology expresses our expectancy of a response to our prayer, because ultimately everything rests in God.

The Lord's Prayer begins and ends with praise to God. This praise articulates a resolute trust in the One who answers our prayers and who alone deserves honor and glory.

> For your journal: In what ways could you incorporate transforming gratitude into your day-to-day living?

In terms of the ladder structure, the doxology also fits beautifully. The prayer begins with careful and direct address to the Father, who

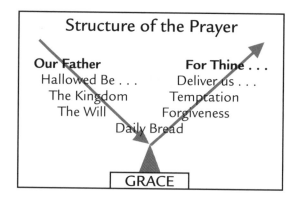

Structure of the Prayer

Our Father / For Thine . . .
Hallowed Be . . . / Deliver us . . .
The Kingdom / Temptation
The Will / Forgiveness
Daily Bread

GRACE

Invocation
The Name
The Kingdom
The Will
Daily Bread
Forgiveness
Temptation
Deliverance
Doxology

seeks relationship with us. The person who prays fills his or her heart and mind and emotions with adoration—seeking God's name, His kingdom, and His will.

The prayer then descends into the requirements of living in a world fractured by sin. It acknowledges that God is the source of all we need: bread, forgiveness, and striking deliverances.

Marjorie Suchocki declares, "There is a movement from gratitude for what we have received, to gratitude for what we know, to gratitude that simply loses itself in God."[1] Gratitude lost in God is authentic worship.

> If there were a "heavenly trust meter" measuring from 0 to 100, where do you think you would register on that scale when you pray?

INSIGHTS FROM THE TEXT

The doxology begins with the little word "for" (the Greek word can also be translated "because"). This conjunction, however, is far from insignificant. It proclaims the reason we can pray and live the Lord's Prayer. It announces the foundation for our confident trust in all the grand requests we have just made.

> In your small group discuss the meaning of "kingdom" in the doxology.

The reason we can pray is because the Kingdom and the power and the glory are not ours, but they belong to God. God is dependable, and Jesus is the reliable partner who teaches us to pray this way.

"Yours"/"to You"—Acknowledgement of Ultimate Ownership

The Greek structure of the doxology has an elegant simplicity. Immediately after the opening, "because" is the possessive pronoun ("to you"/"yours"), acknowledging that God is the ultimate resource for every-

> For the next 14 days, let the doxology be a spontaneous prayer all through your day. Discover as many ways as you can for the use of this doxology during these two weeks. For example, when you face a challenge, let it be your prayer of assurance.

thing. Just as "Father" was first in the sentence structure of the invocation, now the pronoun referring to God is in the premier position. In Greek, the sentence structure underlines the God-centered nature of prayer. The literary structure of the prayer, and the sentence structure of the invocation and doxology all point to the foundational primacy of the God to whom prayer is directed.

"The Kingdom"—Repeating a Primary Theme

"Kingdom" is the only major word that appears twice in the prayer. Both its repetition and its place as the first word of this trio of words ("kingdom," "power," and "glory") underline its importance.

William Barclay argues that the petition for the coming Kingdom is the central petition in the whole prayer because it was our Lord's central message. The parables clearly reveal the value of the Kingdom. The Kingdom is worth any effort (Matt. 11:12), worth any price (parable of the pearl of great price, Matt. 13:45-46), worth any sacrifice (loss of a hand or an eye or a foot is preferable to forfeiting the Kingdom, Matt. 18:8-9). And yet Jesus declares it is a mystery.

> What do you see of the Kingdom that causes you to rejoice and sing praise to God?

At His trial before Pilate, Jesus declared that His kingdom was not of this world. Thielicke, in his sermon on the doxology, says the Kingdom can be understood only from within. He uses the analogy of stained glass windows in a cathedral. From the outside in the daytime they do not disclose beauty. But once you step inside the cathedral, the radiance is visible.

When we begin to see the Kingdom from inside, praise is the only appropriate response. "The kingdom of God is the place where the eternal liturgy is sung, the place of unceasing praise to God."[2]

"And the Power"—the Redefinition of Power

Just as our Suffering-Servant Lord refocused the nature of kingship and Kingdom, He also redefined power. His life and ministry occurred in the context of the Roman Empire, with Caesar playing god. This kingdom was spread across the whole known world with the famous Roman peace controlled by a tyrant.

The arrogant ruthlessness of Caesar power is replaced by servant leadership. The fragile balance of terror is replaced by love. "For the Son of Man came not to be served but to serve, and to give his life a ransom for many" (Mark 10:45).

At the heart of this power is a cross. That cross "disarmed the rulers and authorities" (Col. 2:15), rescued us from death in sins, and "made us

> When did you first become aware of the concept of 'eternal'? Describe the experience in your journal. Then finish this sentence: Today the term "forever" means . . . It makes a difference in my life by . . .

alive together with him" (Eph. 2:5). Hebrews designates this power as "the power of an indestructible life" (7:16). All other powers are ultimately self-destructive.

The doxology ascribes all power and empowerment to God. Recognizing our helplessness, we truly depend on God and, as a result, praise Him.

"And the Glory"—the "Doxological Attitude"

The combination of Kingdom and power and glory is a wonderful hymn of praise to the Creator who redeems us.

The announcement of Jesus' birth was accompanied by an angel choir with the glory of the Lord shining around them. In the introduction to our Lord, John writes, "The Word became flesh and lived among us, and we have seen his glory, the glory as of a father's only son, full of grace and truth" (John 1:14). In John 17 our Lord prays, "Now, Father, glorify me in your own presence with the glory that I had in your presence before the world existed" (v. 5). A few verses later He prays, "The glory that you have given me I have given them, so that they may be one, as we are one" (v. 22). What reality our Lord brings to us!

As we meditate on the transfer of glory from our Master to us, we realize glory belongs only to God. "We end the prayer by reminding ourselves that we are in the presence of the divine glory; and that means that we must live life in the reverence which

> Listen to a recording of "And the Glory of the Lord" from Handel's *Messiah,* or read Isa. 40:1-5). Then record your thoughts, insights, and reflections in your journal.

never forgets that it is living within the splendour of the glory of God."[3]

"Forever"—a Never-Ending Symphony of Praise

"It was customary in later Judaism to add the words 'for ever' (literally 'for the ages') to every ascription of praise to God."[4] These words confess that the Creator God, who set all things in motion, is also the sovereign God who rules beyond the boundaries of time. Nothing can thwart His purposes. So the words "forever" are "set like a seal on the Doxology"[5] and on the whole prayer.

The Great "Amen"—Personalizing the Prayer in Community

I enjoy Malotte's musical setting of the Lord's Prayer. As the doxology builds to the great crescendo in the music, my own heart ascends. The joyous thunder of the final "Amen!" sends shivers up my spine. What a moment!

The word "amen" is phonetically nearly identical across language divisions. In the Hebrew language it derives from the word for truth that signifies firmness, reliability, and certainty.

> The English word "doxology" is derived from the Greek word for "glory."

In Rev. 3:14, in which Jesus is called the "Amen," the next words are "the faithful and true witness, the origin of God's creation." The connection between the name and a reliable promise is clear. Paul writes, "For this reason it is through him that we say the 'Amen,' to the glory of God" (2 Cor. 1:20).

Jesus took this affirmation of the unchangeable nature of God's promises from Jewish worship (where it was most frequently used after a benediction) and placed it at the beginning of some of His most profound promises (doubled for emphasis in the Gospel of John—"Amen Amen")—almost equivalent to an oath.

Philip Hughes observes, "The ancient prayer-ending, 'through Jesus Christ our Lord. Amen' is something far more than a mere formula or a convenient formality; on the contrary, it is the true and profoundly significant keystone of all Christian prayer."[6]

Part of the joy of participating in the Great Amen is realizing this is a community event. With our brothers and sisters in the faith, we celebrate our freedom and the stability of faith in Jesus Christ, the Great Amen.

I've been reflecting on the type of Christian who would develop from praying only the doxology. If a person would contemplate the divine presence with such praise, the only conceivable result would be an "attitude of gratitude." A lifelong relationship with God could be nurtured by praying—and living—the doxology alone.

Our Father in Heaven

Based on Isaiah 64:8; Matthew 6:8-13

♩. = 52

1. We are Your chil - dren, so fra - gile and help - less,
2. You know the bur - dens be - fore we can ask You.

Sim - ply Your crea - tures, the dust of the earth; You, the Al -
Full of com - pas - sion, You give ev - 'ry day. You are for -

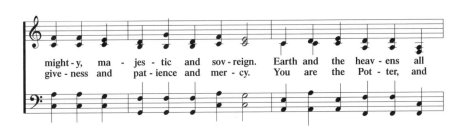

might - y, ma - jes - tic and sov - reign. Earth and the heav - ens all
give - ness and pat - ience and mer - cy. You are the Pot - ter, and

bow to Your Word. We run, Lord, to You, This
we are the clay.

WORDS & MUSIC: Ken Bible

GLORIOUS FATHER
Irregular

mo - ment to You._____ We bow, Lord, and lift up our

hands to You, Fa - ther, Our Fa - ther in heav - en._____

1

2,3 2nd time rit. & Fine

_____ Foun - tain of ho - li - ness, wis - dom and light,

Sea of all good - ness and just - ice and right, Riv - er of

D.S. al Fine

joy and the rich - es of life, Our Fa - ther, our God!_____

13

WHEN PRAYING = LIVING, AND LIVING = PRAYING

*T*he invitation to pray the Lord's Prayer in public often begins with words such as "Would you repeat the Lord's Prayer together?" which implies that saying it is merely a ritual.

At what point in the prayer do you normally check in and really begin praying? Do you fully enter the spirit of prayer with the invocation? Or do you come to prayer at the request for bread? Or does forgiveness grab your attention? Or do temptation and deliverance bring you into the true spirit of prayer? The answer varies in our lives, because this is the prayer for all seasons and all reasons.

The words of Simone Weil sharpen that focus: "The Our Father contains all possible petitions; we cannot conceive of any prayer not already contained in it. It is to prayer what Christ is to humanity. It is impossible to say it once through, giving the fullest possible attention to each word, without a change, infinitesimal perhaps but real, taking place in the soul."[1] Whenever we "check in" while praying the Lord's Prayer, the power of the Kingdom is unleashed, and we are transformed.

THE "SIMPLIFICATION" THESIS

The "simplification" thesis has opened many insights as we have considered each of the petitions in the prayer. The prayer belongs to the core of our Lord's message and life.

If we choose to totally integrate our living and our praying until praying = living, and living = praying, we must take the

> Prayer project: Before arising each morning, pray the Lord's Prayer. Pray it throughout the day in crucial and non-crucial situations. At the end of 30 days, record the impact of this spiritual discipline in your life.

prayer seriously—both the individual petitions and the prayer as a whole. We must feed on this prayer, as Luther said, as a child sucks nourishment from his or her mother. We come to this prayer "not as an escape from responsibility, but as an exercise of Christian freedom and as the beginning of all true knowledge and glad service of God."[2]

If we could uncomplicate our lives to the point that we lived and breathed and prayed only the Lord's Prayer, the focus of our lives would be fully visible. We would be instantly identifiable as servants of the Great Servant in the way we live and pray.

IMPLICATIONS FOR SPIRITUAL FORMATION

It's helpful to see the petitions of the Lord's Prayer as a series of confessions:

1. The invocation is a confession that we are the children of the covenant Father.
2. "Hallowed be thy name" is a confession that only God can finally make His hidden holiness visible.
3. "Thy kingdom come" is a confession that only God can ultimately bring His kingdom into full functioning.
4. "Thy will be done" is a confession that God can accomplish the global reconciling work of His design.
5. "Give us this day our daily bread" is a confession that God is the resource of all resources.
6. "Forgive us" is a confession that the ravages of sin can be reversed only by God's work in Christ at the Cross.
7. "Lead us not into temptation" is a confession of our vulnerability apart from God in the presence of evil.
8. "Deliver us" is a confession that only divine deliverance can replace our own energy and strength.
9. The doxology is a confession of trust in God—in full brass-and-organ crescendo!

In each case the confession sharpens the focus upon God and away from ourselves. We are shaped spiritually by our dependence upon God.

THE LORD'S PRAYER INVITES US TO TAKE GOD SERIOUSLY IN OUR SPIRITUAL FORMATION

The prayer invites us to begin all praying by invoking the Father's blessing. As "Father" is the first word of the prayer in Greek, it should be the very first word in all prayer.

The prayer further instructs us to spend the first major segment of all praying focusing on the God we serve. In the Lord's Prayer in Greek, 55 percent of the words focus on God and only 45 percent on our own needs. This suggests a pattern for praying that I designated the "55/45 split." I often wonder what difference we would see in the spiritual formation of congregations and individuals if we regularly observed this proportion.

THE LORD'S PRAYER INVITES US TO TAKE SIN SERIOUSLY IN OUR SPIRITUAL FORMATION

The Lord's Prayer moves from the grandeur of the divine presence to the struggle of a sin-contaminated world.

Sin is the primary hindrance to spiritual formation. The Bible shows us a devastating picture of the desolation sin has created. The relationships of God and His people are distorted. People's relationships to each other are perverted. Paul observes that sin has contaminated all of creation until "the whole creation has been groaning in labor pains" (Rom. 8:22), anticipating God's redemption.

The Lord's Prayer moves to the heart of the problem by emphasizing forgiveness. The longest and most complex petition is a request for transformation that only divine forgiveness can make.

Sin and evil appear at the close of the Lord's Prayer, put into their proper place as subordinate parasites to the merciful, gracious God and the creation which is filled with his glory. . . . Sin and evil are transient flares against the vast ocean of divine holiness and love. . . . The steadfast love and holiness of the Lord stands forever, inviolable and eternal.

—Timothy Bradshaw
Praying as Believing, 190

The Lord's Prayer ends with petitions for deliverance from evil and the evil one—the ultimate rescue that hallows God's name. Only when sin is acknowledged and resolved in and through the Cross can we find authentic spiritual formation. The radical optimism of grace in the Lord's Prayer enables us to take sin seriously.

THE LORD'S PRAYER INVITES US TO TAKE GRACE SERIOUSLY IN OUR SPIRITUAL FORMATION

The gift of grace is crucial to all spiritual formation. One simple statement of spiritual formation is this: the Christian is a person molded and formed by grace in order to become a vehicle of grace for others.

Danish philosopher Søren Kierkegaard compared the spiritual life to swimming in 10,000 fathoms of water. We are so dependent upon grace that we could not rescue ourselves if we wanted to. To "swim" in grace is the essence of spiritual formation.

Some of the most profound moments in the dynamics of the module on spiritual formation at Nazarene Theological Seminary occur when students break out of a perspective of works-righteousness into the freedom of grace. John Wesley called such a moment "an evangelical conversion." He observed that many people are converted to Christ long before they are converted to the gospel.

At the center of the prayer is the grace of daily bread. When we confess our total dependence upon God and His grace at the Table, the possibilities of spiritual formation increase.

THE LORD'S PRAYER INVITES US TO TAKE FORGIVENESS SERIOUSLY IN OUR SPIRITUAL FORMATION

The last three petitions of the Lord's Prayer do take sin seriously, but not in a negative mode. The radical optimism of grace anticipates a God-oriented deliverance that will free the one who prays.

Forgiveness is at the heart of this deliverance. The deliverance from evil promised by the final petition of the prayer also flows from Jesus' gracious gift on the Cross. Forgiveness and deliverance are God's answers to the damaging effects of sin in our spiritual formation.

The radical optimism of grace announces that God's work on our behalf goes deeper than any brokenness sin can create. If the petitions for forgiveness and deliverance were missing from the Lord's Prayer, the possibilities for spiritual formation would be dim.

THE LORD'S PRAYER INVITES US TO TAKE COMMUNITY SERIOUSLY IN OUR SPIRITUAL FORMATION

No lone rangers exist in God's kingdom. From the opening pronoun, "our," Jesus teaches us the function of community. The grand petitions for God's holy name, God's holy kingdom, and God's holy will are most visible in community. The petitions for bread, forgiveness, and deliverance are all to be prayed in the plural. The words "I," "me," "my," and "mine" are replaced by "we," "us," "our," and "ours" in the Kingdom.

The function of community in spiritual formation cannot be overstated. In *The Upward Call* the role of community was compared to the redwood trees of California. These giant trees with shallow roots "grow in groves, and the roots of many trees entwine. They stand together against the storms as if to announce to the north wind, 'We stand together. If you are going to take one of us out, you will have to take us all.' . . . Christians are like that too. . . . The holy life is not a journey for solitary souls."[3]

THE LORD'S PRAYER INVITES US TO TAKE EVERYDAY RIGHTEOUSNESS SERIOUSLY IN OUR SPIRITUAL FORMATION

The practice of everyday righteousness is the basic evidence of Christlikeness. Let's let Paul have the last word on this topic:

So, chosen by God for this new life of love, dress in the wardrobe God picked out for you: compassion, kindness, humility, quiet strength, discipline. Be even-tempered, content with second place, quick to forgive an offense. Forgive as quickly and completely as the Master forgave you. And regardless of what else you put on, wear love. It's your basic, all-purpose garment. Never be without it.

Let the peace of Christ keep you in tune with each other, in step with each other. None of this going off and doing your own thing. And cultivate thankfulness. Let the Word of Christ—the Message— have the run of the house. Give it plenty of room in your lives. Instruct and direct one another using good common sense. And sing, sing your hearts out to God! Let every detail in your lives—words, actions, whatever—be done in the name of the Master, Jesus, thanking God the Father every step of the way *(Col. 3:12-17, TM).*

THE LORD'S PRAYER INVITES US TO TAKE PRAYER SERIOUSLY IN OUR SPIRITUAL FORMATION

A life bathed in prayer was the tradition from which our Lord came. He had learned to pray at His mother's knee and in regular participation in the patterns of the synagogue in which He was raised.

His own life and ministry reflect a life committed to prayer. He arose early in the morning to pray and often prayed into the night. He prayed privately and publicly.

> Begin a prayer journal. Record your requests, answers, praises, and progress in prayer.

His words in John 14:13-14 emphasize the seriousness of prayer: "I will do whatever you ask in my name, so that the Father may be glorified in the Son. If in my name you ask me for anything, I will do it."

At the heart of all spiritual formation is prayer, for at its simplest, spiritual formation is a carefully nurtured relationship with God. All additional definition of spiritual formation is commentary on that core truth.

THE LORD'S PRAYER INVITES US TO LIVE THE WAY WE PRAY AND PRAY THE WAY WE LIVE IN OUR SPIRITUAL FORMATION

Carroll Simcox summarizes, "Is my offering of the Lord's Prayer becoming more and more a living of it? A prayer of acting and affirming love? If you can answer Yes, be sure that you are moving in the right direction, and thank God."[4]

ALL I EVER NEEDED TO KNOW ABOUT THE LORD'S PRAYER I LEARNED FROM LARRY

Larry is 42 years old and cannot button a button or zip a zipper. But he knows the Lord's Prayer. His caretaker lets him attend a nearby church.

At the open-altar prayer time in the service, he always comes forward. He and his pastor hold hands across the altar and repeat the Lord's Prayer together. As he prays, his hands relax, and his speech becomes less slurred.

After the prayer he will look into his pastor's eyes and ask, "Pastor, do you understand?"

The pastor says, "No, Larry. I don't understand fully."

Larry observes, "But it works! It always works!"

Larry's face glows with his love for his Abba-Father. As he shuffles down the aisle he repeats in his high-pitched voice, "But it works! It always works!"

The psychiatrists say he doesn't understand, but it makes you wonder!

O God, would you allow us to pray the prayer so often and imprint it so deeply upon our very beings that when we become candidates for the home for the terminally bewildered, our last rational thought will be the prayer! In the name of the Father and of the Son and of the Holy Spirit! Amen!

SUGGESTED SUMMARY STUDY QUESTIONS

1. As you think about the implications mentioned in this chapter, which ones do you take more seriously than others? Are there items that need more growth and attention?
2. In your journal for seven days write a letter to the Lord about one of the topics: confession, God, sin, grace, and so on.

3. In your small group discuss one item per each meeting until all seven are covered.
4. In what ways do you intend to integrate the Lord's Prayer into your daily living? Share them with one other person, and record them in your journal. When do you plan to start?
5. What part of this chapter is most challenging to you?

EPILOGUE

An encounter with the Lord's Prayer in a graduate seminar caught this pastor by surprise. The prayer suddenly took on a whole new meaning. It became less a pattern for praying and more a paradigm for living.

After the seminar, the prayer began to shape the pastor at new levels, unhinging some of the prior interpretations that had been so glibly stated and forcing a different understanding of how the prayer might function in a local church.

What might happen if a community of faith began to seriously let the Lord's Prayer shape the church? How might the prayer work its way into the congregation's thinking, relationships, and ministries?

To help his people grasp the impact of the prayer, the pastor led retreats exploring the Lord's Prayer. Leaders began to examine how the Lord's Prayer could shape them individually, how the atmosphere of the congregation could reflect the work of the Spirit, ways relationships within the church would be affected, and how believers could appropriate the dynamic of this prayer in their individual journeys.

As the church board worked through the prayer, relationships were healed, the church found a more cohesive vision of where they should focus attention in ministry development, and all began to see a renewed hunger for authentic spirituality. Board members asked for the prayer retreat based on the Lord's Prayer to become a standard orientation for new board members.

Leadership training events for staff, lay workers, and ministry leaders focused on the Lord's Prayer. Soon small groups and prayer ministry leaders began to request the opportunity to explore the prayer for themselves and their colleagues.

The prayer became a centerpiece for the church's worship. The church has a multiple-service morning worship schedule, and in one form or another in one or more of the services, the Lord's Prayer is repeated, sung, or referred to weekly.

Prayer has become a matter of increased importance in the church. Small-group prayer cells, prayer seminars and retreats, and periods of intense prayer and fasting have become normal. No major decisions are made without public challenges to the congregation to fervently pray.

Recently a spirit of increased effectiveness in evangelism has characterized the church. While other factors have contributed, the renewal has its roots in the rediscovery of a prayer everyone knew, some deeply appreciated, but few studied. Since an emphasis on the Lord's Prayer has been utilized in the congregation, the Lord's Prayer has become a centerpiece of formation, theological orientation, and spiritual maturity.

At least one congregation believed that Jesus meant it when He said, "When you pray, say, 'Our Father . . .'"

—Jesse Middendorf
General superintendent, Church of the Nazarene

Thanks be to God for His amazing grace, and thanks be to our Lord Jesus Christ, who taught us to pray, and thanks be to the Holy Spirit, who "intercedes with sighs too deep for words" (Rom. 8:26).

Amen!

NOTES

Preface

1. Ken Bible and his wife, Gloria, serve God through Living the Natural Way: Innovative Resources for Drawing People to Christ, 103 E. 127th St., Kansas City, MO 64145

Chapter 1

1. All names have been changed to protect confidentiality. Permission for sharing these stories has been granted.

2. H. G. Wells, "Answer to Prayer," *New Yorker* 12, No. 11, 1 May 1937, 18.

3. Edward Schillebeeckx, *Jesus: An Experiment in Christology* (New York: Seabury Press, 1979), 256 ff.

4. William M. Greathouse, *Wholeness in Christ: Toward a Biblical Theology of Holiness* (Kansas City: Beacon Hill Press of Kansas City, 1998), 9.

5. Dallas Willard, *The Divine Conspiracy: Rediscovering Our Hidden Life in God* (San Francisco: HarperSanFrancisco, 1998), 97.

6. Simone Weil, *Waiting on God*, trans. Emma Craufurd (New York: Harper and Row, 1951), 226-27.

7. Marjorie Suchocki, *In God's Presence: Theological Reflections on Prayer* (St. Louis: Chalice Press, 1996), 113.

Chapter 2

1. Randall Earl Denny, *The Kingdom, the Power, the Glory: Embracing the Mystery of the Lord's Prayer* (Kansas City: Beacon Hill Press of Kansas City, 1997), 23. Cited from *Daily Guideposts: 1982* (Carmel, N.Y.: Guideposts Associates, 1981), 304.

2. Steve Shores, *False Guilt: Breaking the Tyranny of an Overactive Conscience* (Colorado Springs: NavPress, 1993) 5.

3. Wesley D. Tracy et al. *The Upward Call: Spiritual Formation and the Holy Life* (Kansas City: Beacon Hill Press of Kansas City, 1994), 43.

4. Gareth Weldon Icenogle, *Biblical Foundations for Small Group Ministry: An Integrational Approach* (Downers Grove, Ill.: Intervarsity Press, 1994), 127.

5. Maxie Dunnam, *Alive in Christ* (Nashville: Abingdon Press, 1982), 39.

Chapter 3

1. Jan M. Lochman, *The Lord's Prayer*, trans. Geoffrey W. Bromiley (Grand Rapids: Wm. B. Eerdmans Publishing Company, 1990), 19.

2. Frederick Buechner, *Listening to Your Life* (San Francisco: HarperSanFrancisco, 1992), 79.

3. Helmut Thielicke, *Our Heavenly Father: Sermons on the Lord's Prayer*, trans. John W. Doberstein (New York: Harper and Row, 1960), 23.

4. William H. Willimon and Stanley Hauerwas, *Lord, Teach Us* (Nashville: Abingdon Press, 1996), 35.

Chapter 4

1. Dee Freeborn, "Living the Lord's Prayer—Part 1," *Herald of Holiness*, August 1994, 39.

Chapter 5

  1. Thielicke, *Our Heavenly Father*, 55.
  2. Willard, *The Divine Conspiracy*, 26.
  3. Thielicke, *Our Heavenly Father*, 59-60.
  4. G. C. Berkouwer, *The Second Return of Christ* (Grand Rapids: Wm. B. Eerdmans Publishing Company, 1972), 453.
  5. Thielicke, *Our Heavenly Father*, 67.

Chapter 6

  1. G. R. Beasley-Murray, *Jesus and the Kingdom* (Grand Rapids: Wm. B. Eerdmans Publishing Company, 1986), 151.
  2. Lochman, *The Lord's Prayer*, 77.
  3. Thielicke, *Our Heavenly Father*, 73.

Chapter 7

  1. Thielicke, *Our Heavenly Father*, 78.
  2. Lochman, *The Lord's Prayer*, 85 ff.
  3. Ibid., 89.
  4. Dee Freeborn, "Living the Lord's Prayer—Part 3," *Herald of Holiness*, December 1994, 33.
  5. Willimon and Hauerwas, *Lord, Teach Us*, 74.

Chapter 8

  1. Lewis Smedes, *The Art of Forgiving: When You Need to Forgive and Don't Know How* (Nashville: Moorings, 1996), 44.
  2. Frederick Bruner, *The Christ Book* (Waco, Tex.: Word Books, 1987), 251. Emphasis added.
  3. Willard, *The Divine Conspiracy*, 264.
  4. F. Hauck, ΌΦΕΊΛΩ, in *Theological Dictionary of the New Testament* (Grand Rapids: Wm. B. Eerdmans Publishing Company, 1967), 5:561.
  5. A. T. Robertson, *Word Pictures in the New Testament* (New York: Harper and Brothers, 1930), 1:54.

Chapter 9

  1. Permission to share this story was granted by the participant. We have been very careful not to breach confidentiality.
  2. The entire sixth chapter of Matthew is tied together by the underlying theme of pious lying. In each case, pious lying forfeits the grace of God. This is particularly true with reference to forgiveness.
  3. Space does not permit full treatment of the subject of forgiveness. We recommend that you obtain Lewis Smedes' *The Art of Forgiving: When You Need to Forgive and Don't Know How* (Nashville: Moorings, 1996).

Chapter 10

  1. Tracy et al. *The Upward Call*, 138.

Chapter 11

  1. Karl Barth, *Prayer*, 2nd ed., ed. Don E. Saliers from the translation by Sara F. Terrien (Philadelphia: Westminster Press, 1963), 83.
  2. Bruner, *The Christ Book*, 255.

Chapter 12

1. Bruner, *The Christ Book,* 123.
2. Thielicke, *Our Heavenly Father,* 154.
3. William Barclay, *The Beatitudes and the Lord's Prayer for Everyman* (New York: Harper and Row, 1964), 255.
4. E. F. Scott, *The Lord's Prayer: Its Character, Purpose, and Interpretation* (New York: Charles Scribner's Sons, 1951), 110.
5. Ibid.
6. Philip Edgcumbe Hughes, *Paul's Second Epistle to the Corinthians* (Grand Rapids: Wm. B. Eerdmans Publishing Company, 1962), 37.

Chapter 13

1. Weil, *Waiting on God,* 226-27.
2. Daniel L. Migliore in Preface, *The Lord's Prayer: Perspectives for Reclaiming Christian Prayer,* ed. Daniel L. Migliore (Grand Rapids: Wm. B. Eerdmans Publishing Company, 1993), 3.
3. Tracy et al., *The Upward Call,* 135.
4. Carroll E. Simcox, *Living the Lord's Prayer: A Study in Basic Christianity* (New York: Morehouse-Gorham Co., 1951), 102.